Were
Cold
Warriors

Volume Two

Here we go again...

A selection of reviews on Amazon from readers of book 1.

This made me laugh out loud so much my missus gave me strange looks.

Really enjoyed it…. I hope there will be more of the same soon.

I had forgotten the laughs until today. Please do another one.

Loads of memories flooded back …. with laugh out loud moments.

Very funny book…. I do hope that a follow up book is written.

Brilliant book about soldiers in BAOR…. can't wait for volume 2.

A hoot and well worth the purchase!

A great anthology of all those urban myths, rumours and insane true stories I recall from my time in BAOR.

A treasure trove of Cold War history and humour.

Waiting for vol 2 with bated breath.

Compulsive reading.

Those were the days…

But out of all of the reviews I got on Amazon from readers of book 1, this was my favourite…

Some of these were to be honest, gross. Military lads are up for anything, so these tales are not for the faint hearted.

All true. Go and have a look on Amazon. While you're there you can rate it yourself! It always makes me laugh when a book from an ex-fullscrew has a higher ranking than a book from an expensively trained ex-pilot! Jonno DP

This book is dedicated to all the men and women of the NATO and allied Armed Forces who are sleeping in a trench tonight, so we can sleep safe in our beds.

Why I Wrote This Book

I didn't think I would end up doing a second book, honestly, but people just kept sending me stories. One day I was looking at a Facebook thread where someone in the group 'The Final RV' had asked the question,
"OK, stupidest thing you have done in green."
Later I found another thread saying,
"Name one thing that you have done that you don't think anyone else on this page has."
These two questions had well over a *thousand* responses. Then I realised a second book HAD to be done. (By the way, The Final RV was closed down by Facebook, it was THAT good. But there is now a new Final RV and it's just as good as the old one.)
I realised a fundamental truth whilst doing the second book and it started with this: All three services take the piss out of each other, each Corp in the Army takes the piss out of each other, each battalion takes the piss out of each other (and I have discovered the same goes for ships in the Navy, and squadrons in the RAF). This continues on down the chain all the way to YOU, yes YOU personally, taking the piss out of the bloke next to you.
But here is that fundamental truth. We are all basically the same, whether you are a soldier, a sailor or an airman. Whether you are a driver, a gunner, a clerk, whatever. We all seem to have this 'thing' in common. I find it a fascinating question, were we born like this, or did the military make us like this?
This fact that we are all basically the same, and that our experiences are similar is still true if you look back in time. In one of Spike Milligan's memoirs about his time in WW2, he mentions being told to quietly lay a communication

1

cable called Don 5 close to German positions. The cable was on a drum with a square hole in the middle, and rotated around a round spindle. (Google it if you don't believe me, they sell 'em on eBay). So as he laid out the cable near heavily armed Germans it went clankety clank, clankety clank. When I was in the army I laid out Don *10* on a drum with a square hole and a round spindle, clankety clank, clankety clank. As I write this there is probably some poor bastard in Afghanistan trying to quietly lay out Don *15*. Clankety clank, clankety clank.

Not just that, what about officers? When I served in the eighties there was a gulf between officers and non-officers that was not bridged. We never let them into our world, and they never let us into theirs, but after the decades have rolled past, I wonder if we were/are actually all that different? For example, I recently watched an interview with Admiral Sandy Woodward, the man who had overall command of the Falklands task force in 1982 and who was often described as the cleverest man in the navy. He explained to the interviewer that when they arrived at the Falklands they didn't know if the intended anchorage near the landing site had been mined, and he didn't have any minesweepers to check.

"What did you do?" asked the interviewer.

"I sent a ship in to see if it went bang."

"Then what?"

"Well, the first ship didn't, so I sent another one in to see if that went bang. That one didn't either. I now felt confident the intended anchorage hadn't been mined so I sent the rest of the fleet in."

The interviewer then asked what he obviously thought was a killer question. "Isn't that a bit harsh on the crews of those ships?"

Woodward seemed a bit bored with the interviewer and gave a reply that any serviceman would see as someone teasing an ignorant civvy. He replied, "If you can't take a joke, you shouldn't have joined."

This rattled the interviewer, and was one of the few times Woodward's mouth curled up into a smile.

Book one was only about the British Army, and just in the time of the Cold War. The reason for this was pure stupidity on my part, I promise you. I thought that after the Cold War it would be more 'sensible' and therefore less interesting. And of course, I did the RAF and Royal Navy a massive injustice thinking their stories wouldn't be as good. Wrong, wrong, wrong again. So wrong in fact, that by the time this is published I will have no option but to be writing volume three as I got so many great stories. I couldn't fit them all in to one book and I promised the senders they would be published, so book three there will have to be. As long as I can do this writing lark, I will publish everything I have promised to publish. If you have a tale to tell, email me at damonjohnson@zoho.com. If it's any good (and most are) I will include it in book 3.

Hopefully I will have a spoken word version of book 1 done by summer 2021 and a spoken word version of book 2 as soon as possible afterwards. If you enjoy this book (or book 1) please leave me a review on Amazon. Comments on what you thought, or suggestions for future publications will be read by me with interest.

Thanks have to be given to several people for helping with this project. First and foremost are the contributors who sent me stories that are just awesome. Especially ex-infantry, who had some great tales, although it did take ages to transcribe them from the original crayon. (Sorry guys, couldn't resist it.) Secondly my poor wife who once again became a book widow for months while I wrote it, but on the plus side, she has watched every single episode of Midsummer Murders without me complaining. Thirdly, thanks to Frank 'the tank' Alexander for his brilliant cover design, and his advice on how to avoid copyright infringements for images. Finally, thanks once again to one of the nicest and cleverest people I have ever met, Lorraine 'two brains' Lateu for proof reading volume two. (I thought she would decline the request as she did the final proof reading for volume one.) She is genuinely awesome, and I always feel like a small child talking to a grown up when I see her. When she was explaining the final edits for book one she started talking about participles. I think I am reasonably intelligent, but I had no clue what a participle is, I still don't. The silence that followed her explanation told her all she needed to know, so she just gave her kind smile and said, "I am sure it will be ok."

Yes I think she is right. I know some ex-servicemen who are not a stupid as they look, but I would be surprised if they write me emails complaining about participles. When I got home I googled 'Participle, meaning'. I still don't understand. If you want to feel stupid too, try it. So, my brothers and sisters, here are the interesting, funny, disgusting (and sometimes all three) stories that you sent me. I just hope you're proud of yourself! (And I hope you enjoy the participles.)

Johnno DP. Warminster. December 2020.

Barbecue in the vehicle sheds

One hot summer's day the whole regiment had pulled the vehicles out of the hangars to do a quiet bit of vehicle maintenance. We were working on our eight scimitars whilst the rest of the regiment worked on their scorpions. The brake pads on these vehicles were notorious for getting covered in oil, which obviously affects the steering and braking. What you *should* do is remove the pads and rub them down with emery cloth. This takes time and effort though, so what we *actually* did was to burn them clean with petrol (which was easy to get as scimitars and scorpions both have petrol engines), taking care not to overheat them as this would make them brittle and unserviceable.

Enter our hero. He poured some petrol from a full twenty litre jerrican can onto some pads, set fire to them, then stepped back knocking over the jerrican. Unbothered by safety or common sense he had left the jerrican top open, so within seconds a growing river of flames was burning merrily inside the hanger. This was quickly noticed by all his potential victims and everyone started shouting at him to put the top back on. Unfortunately this just caused him to panic and he picked up the jerrican and flung it outside the squadron hanger. It sailed frisbee-like though the air dispensing arcs of flaming petrol at a full 360-degree angle like a giant horizontal Catherine wheel and landed with a thud on the tank park causing a jet of burning petrol to splosh across it. A and C squadrons are now frantically trying to move their vehicles back into their hangers, while B squadron are equally frantically trying to move theirs out. The burning petrol is still gurgling out of the can and runs into the central storm drain which runs the whole length of the tank park between B squadron and A and C squadrons. Over the years these drains had filled up with leaves, oil-soaked rubbish, all sorts of bone-dry combustible material which went up in flames with an audible 'woomf' and emitted thick black smoke adding to the general drama.

Meanwhile, the Adjutant in the nearby admin block looked out of his window, saw the long lines of black smoke billowing from the tank park and hit the camp fire alarm.

Our hero was still running around like a headless chicken getting shouted at by everyone in range when he heard the fire alarm. Because he is on fire picket (being on guard duty that night) he runs off into the sunset to answer the fire call, leaving everyone else to clear up the mess.

Mumble Smith 1RTR

You can always rely on the French...

In late 1982 I was an RO2 on the Aircraft Carrier HMS Hermes and as a reward for being good in the Falklands the Hermes was sent on a jolly (a quick trip to somewhere nice) as a sort of thanks for all you did down south, and to fly the flag in a foreign port to foster good relations etc etc. However, this was not how it turned out. We went to the lovely French town of Brest famous for its wine, its food and the fact the Allies flattened it in World War two. A fact that I think the locals still hadn't quite put behind them.

The day we arrived the locals were holding a pro Argentine rally and we were welcomed by cries of "Vive le

Exocet" which were being chanted over and over. Hermes was tied up in the most faraway place they could get us in the dockyard to try and minimise contact. Not easy for a 28,000-ton ship with a crew of 2,100! It also struck me as a little counterproductive on a publicity trip!

The first night there were running fights in the streets between the crew and the locals. The following night anyone from the ship who could be spared was given leave to go ashore and 'enjoy' themselves. It was even worse than the night before. I remember walking back through the dockyard gates wondering where the French sentry and his oppo were when I heard a faint cry from the bridge over the river. I looked over and saw that both of them were up to their waists in mud, having been flung over by returning drunken Matloes. In the end it got so bad on this 'goodwill trip' that we were asked to leave early. The Hermes had a full crew at the time and there were just too many defaulters for the Captain to get through. To get through it, the defaulters were put in batches of thirty by the first Lieutenant who was sporting a black eye and a CS spray burn on his face. They were marched in, got 'case dismissed' and got marched back out again.

Happy days!

Anon

I'm sure no one will notice...

In the early 1990's at RAF Kinloss we once had a new guy who was given the job of washing the windscreen of a Nimrod aircraft. You would think this was a safe chore for someone as yet unused to working around aircraft, but no. As the windscreens are well above a person's reach, you need a special ladder to do this. He was not a tall guy and once he got to the top of the ladder, he wasn't *quite* able to reach all the way over. Rather than climbing down the ladder and shifting it along a bit he saw a handy tube of metal sticking out of the aeroplane and stood on it so he *could* reach. When he climbed down his ladder he realised that he had bent this handy step that the Nimrod designers had so thoughtfully supplied.

What he had just bent was a pitot probe, which is an airspeed indicator that usefully tells the pilot how fast he is going. This act of laziness had just grounded a multi-million pound aircraft. Being a bit worried about getting into trouble if it was noticed, he stood back to compare the alignment of the probe with the other three Nimrods that were parked up in a line with the one he had just damaged.

It was obviously bent.

With the kind of inspiration that you either admire or shake your head at, he dragged the ladder up to the other three aircraft in turn and bent their probes so it wasn't so obvious that something was amiss. Satisfied with grounding the entire fleet he wandered off, looking for other things to fix presumably. Fortunately for the crews it was noticed and repaired before any of them took off.

We didn't tend to deal with stuff like this by reporting it, we tended to deal with things like this internally without involving officers. He was taken outside for a 'wee chat' from his chief tech that would have left no visible bruises, but would have left him clearly understanding that this was not to happen again. Single handedly, and in minutes, he caused more damage than the Russians ever did.

RAF Anon. (And no, it wasn't me).

Up, up, and ..... leg it!

Me and my best mate Gaz came back in off the piss one night at about 3 ish and Gaz decided he wanted to have a dump in one of the guard boxes on the regimental square. These were just like the ones you see outside Buckingham Palace and the guards seemed to like to practise standing in them. (We shared the camp with a guard's regiment). I don't know why you needed to practise standing in a vertical box, but I suppose you must or they wouldn't have done it. They seemed to like it anyway.

We were not big fans of the Guards, in fact they were a pain in the arse, hence Gaz wanting to shit in one of their sentry boxes. But when we got to the square our attention was drawn to a big dark object smack in the middle of it. Closer inspection revealed it to be a scout helicopter. We wandered around it a bit and then I announced to Gaz, "I know how to fly that!"

"Fuck off" said Gaz.

It was true though. A relative of mine was a helicopter pilot and had flown these for years. He had frequently taken me up when I was a boy and after a lot of trips he started letting me do all the pre-flight checks, and then the start-up routine. After a while he even let me hold the controls and do some gentle manoeuvring. I am being vague about this because although it was years ago I don't want some smart ass coming to find me or my relative, and Jonno DP has promised to 'accidentally' wipe his C drive if it comes to it.

Anyway, we climb aboard and strap ourselves in. I start to do the pre-flight checks through a lager coloured haze and felt pleased that it is all coming back to me. It did take longer than before because there seemed to be twice as many switches and dials as there used to be, but that might have been because I was hammered. The lights were coming on, and the turbine had started. Gaz was impressed and he said so, "Fucking hell, you really do know what you are doing don't you!"

I belched and gave him the kind of smile that James Bond gives M at the beginning of a mission, and flicked a few more switches.

Now here's the thing. When you start up a helicopter you leave the engine running for two minutes without engaging the rotors. This is because a cold engine under load wears a lot more than a warm one. The same is true for all engines, but helicopter engines are really expensive, so it's worth going to the trouble of waiting. I say 'helicopter', I mean 'scout helicopter', as it's the only one my relative flew. You *are* allowed to engage the rotors and take off without waiting for the two-minute engine warm up, but only in time of war or in an emergency.

We had walked onto the square unnoticed.

We had climbed into the helicopter unnoticed.

We had strapped ourselves in unnoticed.

But starting the engine *was* going to be noticed and engaging the rotor blades and starting them rotating would be *very* noticed.

So dear reader, there we are. In a very expensive helicopter, strapped in, headsets on, engine running, pissed as farts, and the people on guard duty are running straight at us.

WHAT??? Oh fuck! The guard are running straight at us!

"Take off!" yelled Gaz.

"I can't!"

"Why not?"

"We have to wait two minutes!"

"Why?"

"'Cos it's not an emergency!"

"I think it fucking is..." This last bit was said over his shoulder as he was getting out of the door and running away.

I did the same. I clambered across, out the door, and legged it about twenty yards ahead of the guys on prowler. Shitfaced though I was, I was surprised at how fast I could run.

We legged it across the square and into an accommodation block. The guys doing the guard duty were from the Guards regiment, and it was one of their blocks we went into. This wasn't a mistake; we were trying to make them think the wannabe helicopter thieves were from their unit and not ours. Thinking about it, it's not just surprising how fast you can run when pissed, it's even more surprising how sneaky you can be when you are pissed. By the time we got inside we had built up a slightly bigger lead and we quietly tip-toe ran across the internal bridge that connected the different accommodation blocks. When we got into ours we dived into our room, and as quick as possible Gaz and I got into our respective pits and feigned sleep. No one disturbed us.

Come Monday morning I, and the rest of my platoon, was marching past the guard room when the provost sergeant came out and told us to halt.

He stood us to attention and machine gunned us with his eyes. "Some fucking arsehole tried to steal a helicopter from the square Saturday night. Does anyone know anything about this?"

Fuck!

"Also, there is only one person in this whole fucking camp that has a relative who flies scout helicopters, and might know how it works."

Fuuuuck!!!

He looked at me and said, "I fucking know you (insert my name here) and I knew your fucking (insert relative here) before he transferred out of the parachute regiment and into the Army Air Corps."

Fuuuuuuuuuuuuuck!!!!!!!!!

I said nothing and tried to look innocent. I shrugged.

Eight years (yes, eight years) later I was on guard duty and found myself in a camp with that provost sergeant, only he was a sergeant major by then. He recognised me and came across smiling.

"Hi mate," he said, "how's things?"

He started chatting away for a bit, then he smiled and said "Hey, do you remember that time someone tried to nick a helicopter from the regimental square?"

I smiled back and gave an 'Aww shucks, it was me' look. I saw anticipation gleam in his eyes.

"Dunno what you are talking about sir."

His mouth hardened into an angry line and then he raved at me for ages shouting "I fucking know it was you! Admit it" etc etc. I never did though.

The only 'trouble' I got in over the incident was when I was in a pub with (insert relative here), who had been the one who taught me to fly it, and I told him, step by step, what I had done. He listened in silence and when I finished he said, "You fucking asshole!"

Shocked and a bit offended I asked why. He took a swig from his pint and said, "You forgot to check the engine oil."

Definitely Anonymous

"Don't live the same year 75 times and call it a life."

Robin Sharma

An Airborne invasion

Not all REME spend their time fixing things, sometimes we do get some interesting postings. In 1960/61 I was a corporal and got attached to 12 Brigade Royal Military Police on the German North Sea island of Sylt. Back then the RMP had had quite a big role, and we were policing a big airborne invasion exercise by Aldershot's finest, the parachute regiment. We had to be careful with our dealings with the locals as Sylt was even then a popular tourist destination for Germans.

The RMP had their work cut out as boy, do those paras do know how to unwind! There was a nightclub in the town, called Le Pigalle, which was out of bounds to squaddies, but as is to be expected, the proprietor was always outside encouraging them in. However, once they had paid the expensive cover charge to get in, the owner would look for any reason to chuck them out. If you are not familiar with the mentality of 'The Maroon Machine' I can tell you from personal experience it is not in a paratrooper's nature to quietly accept things they see as unfair, so they would refuse to leave. So the owner would call the local Polizei who didn't fancy mixing it with the paratroopers and they would call in the RMP and the 'troublesome' paras would have a ding dong with the RMP before being chucked out. This was an outrage in several ways as he was making all the cash, the paras were being ripped off and the RMP were having to do all the legwork. I was working as a Mobile Patrol Driver in an Austin champ with a VERY big Jock RMP and on one particular evening that we were in town he grabbed two small Glaswegian Paras, one in each hand, and asked them if they fancied a fight. Of course, being both paras and Glaswegian they readily agreed.

"Right." said the huge RMP, "Get a few of your mates and go into Le Pigalle and beat it up good. From the moment you start, there will be no police in the town for twenty minutes."

As he was a fellow Jock, they took him at his word, and we went back to base for a coffee break. We had no sooner started sipping from our mugs when the phone rang. Looking at our watches we gave it 20 minutes, then drove back into town.

On our arrival we were surprised to find there were no paras about at all, but every one of Le Pigalle's windows were broken and most of the bar's furniture was outside, smashed to pieces, on the pavement. The male staff of Le Pigalle had fled in the face of the airborne onslaught, but being gentlemen, the paras had secured all of the ladies in a back room for their safety whilst they trashed the place.

We got another call from the Polizei one sunny afternoon about a week later. It was to complain about a group of paras performing company drill on the local nudist beach dressed (only) in boots and red berets.

It was time for coffee break again.

Ron Allen REME

A privileged position

Many years ago I was working in a small comcentre in London and one of our duties was to carry out various signals duties for the parades and ceremonies that occurred in the city.

In earlier years, should a guardsman faint during the Trooping of The Colour he would be left on the Horseguards Parade ground to recover for some time until finally collected by stretcher bearers. This naturally led to many complaints from the general public, so the Headsheds decided to modernise the procedure. This wish to modernise culminated in three Royal Signals personnel being equipped with radios and put in key locations. One was positioned in a room overlooking the parade, one located near St James Park with the stretcher bearers and a third, me in this case, was positioned in the bay on the north side of the Horseguards triple archways.

The idea was that the observer in the room would see and note the position of any fainting guardsmen during the ceremony and he would report "Casualty, third rank 2nd Battalion Grenadier Guards" for example. This verbal message would pass via my radio relay directly to the stretcher team who would immediately dash onto the parade and 'remove the inert soldier in a smart, efficient and soldierly manner' as the Garrison RSM would say. My radio was the back-up for the relay. On the right-hand side of me were the scaffold stands holding the thousands of general public who were going to watch the parade.

Of course we had rehearsed the parade routine several times. The Household Cavalry, after completing their part of the ceremony, carefully backed their horses into the bays either side of the Horseguards archways and my view

17

of the parade was therefore blocked by two very large horses' backsides. As I said this did not matter as my task was just the radio relay, not an observer.

The actual day of the ceremony was quite warm and dry. Ideal for Her Majesty to enjoy the really wonderful parade in her honour and of course the grandest part of the ceremony, the Trooping of a guard regiment's colours. Because I was part of the occasion I was wearing my Royal Signals No. 1 Dress uniform, (Blues).

Unfortunately the only casualty of the day appeared to be me. As the horses backed carefully into the bay they came within a couple of feet of my position. Suddenly the huge animal directly in front of me decided to have a leisurely but forceful pee and, being a mare, gracefully lifted her tail and jetted me with very warm, very yellow piss! Of course the audience in the stands to my right heard and saw this happen, much to their delight!

I was less chuffed.

Naturally I could not leave my position until the parade was complete and I remained pissed-upon and dripping until her majesty decided to nip off for tea and buns with the gang at Buck House. The Landrover driver took me home holding his nose as I steamed quietly in the back; he would not let me sit in front. I tried to bill the army for dry cleaning...

Unsuccessfully I might add!

John R. Royal Signals

Things you thought you knew #1

The SA80 type rifle is a modern idea

The SA80 is a 'bullpup' type of rifle, meaning the moving parts are behind the trigger. The first prototypes of the SA80 were created in 1976 and the weapon started to be issued in the late 1980's, ending in 1994 when the A2 variant replaced the A1. The A2 variant came to be as the result of a significant upgrade in the early 2000s by Heckler & Koch and the A3 variant was first issued in 2018 with several more improvements.

But the British were not the first country to issue a weapon of this type. In 1978, the Austrian Army became the first military force in the world to adopt a bullpup rifle, the Steyr AUG (Army Universal Gun), as its principal combat weapon. Since then the militaries in many countries have followed suit, such as Australia, China, India, Israel, France, Singapore and of course Britain.

But all of this well-known history obscures an incredible fact. The bullpup design goes back to 1901! And it is, of course, British.

The so called 'Thorneycroft carbine' was the earliest of all the bullpup designs and was developed by the James Baird Thorneycroft company in 1901. It was a bolt action rifle in which the bolt slid back through the butt of the weapon almost touching the shoulder. The ammunition was the standard .303 round and the rifle had a five round magazine.

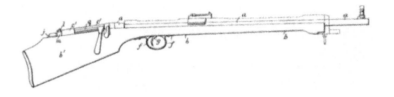

The Thorneycroft carbine 1901

The Thorneycroft carbine was about 20 centimetres shorter and almost 10% lighter than the standard issue .303 Lee–Enfield which was in service at the time, but at trials in Hythe it was decided that there was excessive recoil, and the long serving .303 Lee-Enfield was kept.
So what? You may be thinking, as far as modern weapons go, we are back to the start of this story, i.e. the 1970's. No. Incredibly, there was the EM1 and the EM2 which were designed by Britain in the 1940's, and the EM2 actually started to go into service in the 1950's!
Both weapons were named after their chief designers, the EM1 being known as the Thorpe rifle and the EM2 the Janson rifle. Odd though this story is, it gets odder. The chief designer of the EM2, the British army's first assault rifle, was a man called Stefan Kenneth Janson. This is the anglicised name of the Polish firearm designer Captain Kazimierz Januszewski. So with the Cold War starting to really bite, the best weapon we had was designed by an East European! As well as the EM1 and EM2, an EM3 and EM4 were also being worked on, but they got no further than the drawing board.

The EM1 bullpup assault rifle.

The EM2 bullpup assault rifle.

So why did Britain throw away a thirty-year head start on the world in advanced small arms design, and abandon the project? In short, politics, money and American influence. The EM2 was briefly adopted as the British Army's new rifle on 25 April 1951 but this decision was quickly reversed by Winston Churchill's incoming government as he was very interested in getting standardisation of NATO ammunition and if possible, weapons.

The EM2 used the highly efficient short 7.1mm round, which had been designed to replace the time honoured .303 round which had been in use for over fifty years. However, the US disagreed with the British and pushed for the adoption of the 7.62 × 51mm NATO round for two reasons. Firstly, they claimed the British 7.1 round was too weak for use in assault rifles and machine guns and secondly, they didn't want to acknowledge the superiority of the British round and undermine their own manufacturing dominance.

The British disagreed and said that the 7.62mm round was too powerful to be used in fully automatic assault rifles as the more powerful recoil meant that after the second round was fired you wouldn't be shooting with any meaningful accuracy. In the end, the British were proved right. The 7.62mm round *was* too powerful for fully automatic assault rifles and the Americans adopted the 5.56 round which was not. As the calibre of the EM2 could not be easily adapted, and the British government was still seeking standardisation of ammunition within NATO, it was scrapped.

Now the bullpup designs were off the table, the only reasonable alternative for Britain was to buy the Belgian made FN FAL rifle which came to known as the SLR. As all British service personnel who used it know, the SLR takes the 7.62 × 51mm NATO round which the Americans had initially, and incorrectly, insisted upon as the standard ammunition for fully automatic NATO assault rifles. Churchill hoped that with Britain, the Commonwealth and other NATO countries all adopting the FN FAL the US Army would do so as well. However, the US initially adopted the

T44 (an updated version of the M1 Garand) and called it the M14. Due to combat experience in Vietnam, the US had to admit what the British had been saying all along, the 7.62 round *was* too powerful for a fully automatic assault rifle, and they adopted the 5.56 × 45mm NATO intermediate cartridge for their M16's which was less powerful than the British 7.1mm round that had been dismissed as not powerful enough.

Around 1970, a pair of the original 7.1mm EM-2 rifles were re-barrelled for an experimental 6.25mm cartridge but this project was soon dropped for an even smaller 4.85mm cartridge in a completely new rifle, the L64/65 which evolved into the 5.56mm SA80 currently used by the British Army.

L64/65 assault rifle

It's easy to be critical of the people making the decisions back in the 1950's and 1960's, and even more so if you think about other examples of British inventive genius that could have been pursued like the British space programme or the TSR2 fighter aircraft, both of which were cutting edge at the time. But it has to be remembered that the Second World War had left Britain virtually bankrupt and highly dependent on the United States. Britain didn't finish repaying World War Two loans to them (and the Canadians) until 2006! At least some of the astoundingly brilliant military projects did get through, like the HMLC Stalwart ammunition carrier in the army and the Harrier jump jet, both of which are in a class of their own.

The SA80 has now been in service for over thirty years, so whilst it has not yet attained the venerability of the Lee Enfield .303 and its variants, the time must soon be approaching for the next generation. I hope its lasers!

Researched and written by Jonno DP

"Every man thinks less of himself for not having been a soldier."

Samuel Johnson

The Chinese Cold War

The Chinese shared the Russian ambition for a world painted red. They used different methods though, like the Korean and Vietnam wars and riding on the back of the Malay emergency and the Borneo confrontation. When I was in Hong Kong they planted bombs, set up riots, and constantly threw threats across the border.

I was in charge of inspections in the Ordnance Depot around 1967/68 and every six months I had to take myself and one other up to the mountainous restricted border area at Sek Kong and check about twenty Centurion tanks (ex-Korean war) stored in light preservation. Whilst up there we had to do visual checks and give them a run out leaving a task sheet of faults for the mechanics based there.

One beautiful sunny day I decided that they were due a longer, tougher exercise. I cleared it with the range warden and we set off in the first one over a nice looking mountain. I drove and my corporal was commanding but as the radios were stored separately we had no intercom. Now, if you are too young to know, Centurions had a huge 27 litre petrol engine called the Meteor, a brother to the famous Merlin engine used in Spitfire and Hurricane fighters. As the engine was not connected to an aircraft propeller to keep the revs down, it needed an engine governor. This governor worked by cutting the ignition for a few moments, and thereby cutting the engine out, but it did not cut the fuel (do you see where we are going here?). When this happened a large amount of unburnt vapourised petrol would be going down a very hot exhaust pipe and when it reaches the end... a backfire, and a big one!

So we came over the top of the mountain and fifty tons of tank was suddenly able to roll down the other side. As the Cent starts going down the hill part of my brain noticed a film set on the road at the bottom. It was a Chinese version of Romeo and Juliet and the heroes were fleeing from the nasty Baron's evil cavalry in a stage coach. The plan was that as the coach reached a bend in the track a stunt man hiding in a hole in the ground would pull a pin holding the horses and the carriage together thus detaching the two. The horses would keep running and coach would run up a ramp and stop. Unfortunately for this Chinese George Lucas, whilst this stunt was being attempted the governors on my Cent cut in. Two huge bangs were accompanied by six-foot flames from both exhausts and all the horses set off at a world record speed. The driver fell off the coach, the cavalry horses fled in all directions shedding their riders, and the cowardly stunt man hid in the bottom of his hole. Last seen, the now out of control coach was bouncing over the top of the next mountain, with the stars in each door, trying to pluck up the courage to jump. I went down to apologise to the director thinking he would be furious. He said, "Don't worry sir, we have it all on film, I will use it in my next production."

A few days later, we were to go back to Sek Kong to inspect the remaining tanks but my mate's wife called in to say that he was sick. I had three Chinese Inspectors who worked with me, one of them (actually called Sky Fer) volunteered. He cheerfully told me that he, "Drive many tanks, I do all for you here."

Ok, off we go. All British tanks steer through the transmission. A good system, but it's important for the driver to look ahead and select the correct gear to obtain the radius needed to get around a corner. When we got to Sek Kong, and he saw how big they were, he needed all his Chinese inscrutability to cover his doubts. Up to this point he hadn't mentioned that he had only driven Comets on the road, which were much smaller and lighter. We started off with him driving and me sitting on the front showing him the way. (I should have been in the turret, but as we had no intercom I had to sit on the front to give him directions.) We were following a track around the side of a mountain and the bend was tightening up. He needed to change down. I looked at him and he smiled at me. "Change down!" I shouted.

He smiled.

"Quick! Change down!!!" I shouted louder.

Oblivious, he just smiled until we became airborne off the steep side of the mountain. Tanks do fly, but what a crash! I blacked out for a moment, then came to. We were in the middle of a huge chicken farm. Me and the tank were completely covered in white feathers and chicken shit! Skiver had ducked down inside.

I did not let him drive again.

Ron Allen REME

Barred!!

Around Christmas 1990 I was working behind the bar in the officers Mess in the Falklands which was a good job if you liked your booze and even better if you liked it free. Some days we would crack our first tin at 10am. Mick Miller and some other comedian that I had never heard of were booked to do a combined services show in the Mess, which I thought was great as I had seen Mick Miller and thought he was funny. Mick Miller comes on wearing a tuxedo and was doing his really funny stand up whilst me and my Corporal, Shady Adie, (so called because he often used to wear a pair of expensive Ray-Ban wayfarers), were behind the bar and thinking this was pretty cool, free booze and a free show. And you never know, we might get the chance to meet the comedians after.

In the Falklands at that time all beers were colour coded. For example, Becks was green, Carlsberg was blue, McEwan's export was red etc. There were only about five beers available and people just asked for the colour rather than the actual name.

We were both enjoying the show as all of the customers had got their drinks in (so had we, several) and were merrily laughing along at the routine. Irritatingly, this weird looking bloke turns up and asked for drinks. In a high pitched voice he said "I will have a tin of red, a tin of green…"

This wasn't funny. He was putting on this weird voice, and it just pissed Adie and me off. We couldn't concentrate on the show whilst we were being distracted by this bloke who thought he was some kind of comedian.

Mightily irritated I gave him my thousand yard stare. "You fucking what?" I said flatly.

In the same high pitched squeaky voice that was no funnier second time around than it was the first, "I will have a tin of red, a tin of green..."

I cut him off by turning to Adie and saying, "Hey Adie, there is some fucking bloke over here that is taking the piss."

Without taking his eyes off the stage Adie asked, "Is he pissed?"

"Dunno"

Reluctantly dragging his attention away from Mick Miller Adie looked at me and said "Oh fuck him off. What rank is he?"

"I think he's a civvy."

"Get him the fuck out if he's taking the piss."

The piss taker wasn't particularly tall, but he was pretty big built. I went around the bar and squared up to him. "You! Fuck off now!"

He started to protest but I wasn't having it, especially as he kept up that annoying silly voice, so out he went. About ten minutes later Mick Miller had finished his routine and came up to the bar. "Scuse me guys, have either of you seen the other guy who's with me?"

"Who's that then?" I asked.

"Big guy, squeaky voice. He's called Joe. Joe Pasquale"

"Oh."

"What?"

"I threw him out about ten minutes ago."

"Why?"

"I thought he was taking the piss with his squeaky voice."

We went outside and found Joe Pasquale who had been standing in the car park wondering what to do. After I had apologised, we let him back in.

He got his revenge though. A couple of days later he was doing his show for the NCO's and OR's and he said "Where's that fucking wanker who kicked me out of the officer's mess the other day?"
What else could I do? I stood up and waved.

SAC Mike 'Bert' Eisinger. RAF.

"Pain is the feeling of weakness leaving the body."

Ten thousand Army PTI's.

In the crap as usual

The RSM asked me, "Do you want to be an RSM one day?"
I told him I wouldn't mind having his wages for a month or
two. He seemed to lose his friendliness at this point and
repeated through gritted teeth, "I said, do you want to be
an RSM one day?"
After confirming that one day I hoped to achieve the top
position of RSM, he replied, "Good! Now report to the
TCO (Transport Control Officer) of 36 Sqn and pick up the
rubbish truck, you are now the Regimental Shit Mover."
(RSM – get it?) The rubbish truck was an old Bedford RL
tipper truck that had a superstructure and canvas cover on
the back, just like the troop-carrying version, but with a
shorter wheelbase. The rear main body could be elevated
to tip out the rubbish by means of a hydraulic pump
powered by the engine. The job of 'Regimental Shit
Mover' was actually quite a doddle of a job. I was my own
boss and as long as I emptied all the dustbins around the
camp, no one ever bothered me. Another reason I wasn't
pestered by the Regiment very much was because I
smelled like a Victorian dustbin most of the time. It was
hard work on a Monday morning though. The dustbins
were always overflowing with empty food wrappers, beer
bottles and discarded porno magazines, usually with the
pages stuck together. Squaddie weekends rarely varied.
I had been doing the job for about two months when the
TCO informed me that Driver Ainsworth was to take over
from me. He had to work with me for a couple of days to
learn the locations of all the dustbins around the camp
and where the landfill sites were. We reported to the Pay
Office and picked up a chit that had to be handed in every
time we dropped a load at the rubbish dump. The

'Obercrappensitenführer' at the dump in Bielefeld would regularly say to me, "Kein Chit, Kein shit" (No Chit, No Shit). On my last day, we had about half a load of garbage in the truck when I was passing 9 Squadron accommodation block and I decided to show Ainsworth where the bins were on the other side of the main drill square. As I turned left onto the square, I saw 9 Squadron, 17 Squadron, and 36 Squadron, smartly lined up on an RSM's Parade. The Commanding Officer was standing on his dais at the front of the Regiment, prepared to take the salute when they all marched past. The moment the tyres of my rubbish truck defiled the RSM's parade ground he blew a gasket. I could tell he wasn't happy because he started waving his pace stick at me in a threatening manner and his face turned a dark shade of puce. The language he spewed out probably shouldn't have been used in front of the CO.

"DRIVER CLACY! GET THAT FUCKING HEAP OF FUCKING SHIT OF MY FUCKING PARADE GROUND BEFORE I FUCKING JAIL YOU!"

Keen to comply with the RSM's wishes, I put my foot down and accelerated as quickly as I could so I could get off his blessed parade ground PDQ (Pretty Damn Quick). As I approached the CO, Driver Ainsworth got out of his seat and stood to attention on the engine cover with his top half out of the cupola in the roof of the cab. Whilst I sped past the rear of the dais, Ainsworth did a smart salute to our Commanding Officer. The Lieutenant Colonel returned his salute and pirouetted whilst doing a good impression of a guppy fish. What a stirring sight we must have made! I was later told that the canvas on the truck was flapping about like Batman's cape and due to the rapid acceleration, all sorts of rubbish was flying out the back of the truck.

Oops! Sorry sir!

Harry Clacy 10 Regiment RCT Bielefeld

This story also appears in Harry Clacy's excellent book 'Harry was a Craphat'.

Not a mortal wound

Being the nig who's just arrived at your unit is one of the most uncomfortable experiences I ever had as a soldier. But at least I comforted myself with the thought that I would not be the new guy for long. Little did I know that my unit was about to be amalgamated with another regiment and they wouldn't be sending any more nigs, which would leave me as the nigiest of the nigs, for two-and-a-half years. It did have an unexpected upside though. About a year after I arrived in Germany (this was either late 83 or early 84) my TSM called me into his office and said that they had been asked to send volunteers to act as simcas (simulated casualties) on an exercise for the Royal Army Medical Corps. As we were not that busy as a unit I could definitely be spared. In fact, in the words of my troop Sergeant I was a useless cunt, so I may as well go. Thanks sarge.

I was told to go to the QM's and draw old combat jackets, trousers etc that had been exchanged as worn out or damaged so they could be ripped when simulating battle wounds. The storeman tried to mark all the stuff so I couldn't bring it back and exchange it later but I made the most of the opportunity and got tons of kit that I immediately removed his marks from. Cheers easy.

Off I went to this field hospital with a large pack, a Sven Hassel paperback and a carton of Benson and Hedges. I had been told I wouldn't need much kit because I'd be spending most of my time in bed anyway.

When I got there I met one of the funniest characters it's ever been my luck to be in the same room as. I wish I could remember his name, but this is forty years ago. I do remember he was an artilleryman like me though. He had a thick north Eastern accent and everybody just called him Geordie. My regiment had its recruiting area in the northeast of England so I was familiar with the character of the people coming from that part of Britain and unlike many of the medics on the exercise I could understand what he was saying, having learnt over the past year how to translate from Geordie into English.

Examples:
- Howk – to pick or scratch
- Haddaway and shite – go away, you are talking rubbish.
- Toon – Newcastle united
- Ya'aalreet – how are you

I am not kidding either. He had an accent so thick you could stir it with a stick, and several medics required my translation services. If you're not familiar with this strange race of people I will tell you what they're like. Generally speaking of course, Northeasterners were open, trustworthy, tough, friendly, but most of all very, very funny. I've never met any people from anywhere else in Britain who are so hell-bent on having a good time. And I do mean that sentence literally. I was always amazed at how many north easterners there were that would just spontaneously think 'This seems funny, let's do it,' with absolutely no consideration for the consequences.

When I met Geordie in that field hospital I'd met a master of the art. He even looked funny, and he looked funnier still standing next to me. Where I was short, he was tall. Where I had unremarkable brown hair close cut, he looked like Worzel Gummidge on a windy day. Where I was quiet, he was a FUCKING LUNATIC. Where I spoke quietly his voice boomed. Where I would draw the line at being in too much trouble, he was a FUCKING LUNATIC. He had a smile that on anyone else might have been disarming but on him was simply frightening. This is mostly because his two top front teeth were missing and when he smiled it looked like you were making him hungry. It was the kind of look that made people back off and reach for any available weapon. He also had the odd quirk that if he agreed with you and said "Aye" (which is Geordie for yes if you didn't know) or "Why aye" (which is an even stronger affirmative) he would nod his head to the side and one of his eyes closed slightly giving the overall impression that he was winking at you. Looking back now I think he might have been a bit deaf as well which was why he spoke so loudly. He genuinely thought he was just being enthusiastically friendly but he came across as somebody with a loose hinge. Maybe the person who recruited him was in his last week at the recruitment office and just didn't give a shit anymore.

I was looking forward to chatting up the pretty nurses but the army isn't as stupid as we hoped. This senior nurse who we were going to be dealing with was amazing. I don't know what rank she was but looking back at how she behaved I'm guessing it was something like Sturmbannführer. Why she became a nurse I will never know. She was completely unfriendly, un-gentle, un-nurse like and looked like Winston Churchill in drag. Only less feminine.

The most off-putting thing about her was that she spoke in a strange kind of deep male voice with a squeaky edge to it, the kind of voice that someone who is new to transvestism uses. After she directed us to get into the army issue pyjamas and get into bed, she left the room with scarcely another word. As soon as the door closed Geordie turned to me, smiled, raised one eyebrow and said "Ee Jannah, di ye naa thas a fookin blerke tharris!" (Hey Jonno, do you know what? That's a fucking bloke that is!) I tried arguing that the army hasn't got a sense of humour that sophisticated, but he looked at me with the smug expression of someone who has seen through a con trick. He really was convinced that Nurse Churchill was a man.

In the afternoon we lined up to get our simulated wound and Nurse Churchill was there to victimise, I mean supervise. She spotted us and steamed over with a malicious gleam in her eye. When we got to the front she checked a clipboard and said to the person putting the fake wounds on:

"Ah yessss….. shrapnel wound, buttocks".

Geordie exploded in his native gibberish, fortunately not understood by the medical crew present, and it took me a while to calm him down and persuade him that she had said 'buttocks' and not 'bollocks'.

I was hoping for something a little more heroic to impress any attractive nurses with, but now Geordie and I were going to be left showing our skinny white asses to every female who came within range, which was not my best feature. At this point I was probably still underestimating

Geordie and Nurse Churchill certainly was. In contrast to my shyness when my 'wound' was to be checked by medics, whenever any medical staff came near Geordie he would whip the blanket off and with a hearty cry shout "There you gan marra". The more he acted up, the more Nurse Churchill would try to make his life difficult in some way, and the more he would wind her up. The point at which Nurse Churchill definitively lost the battle came a day or so later. I think she realised then that not only was Geordie not going to give in but he was not capable of giving in.

Boredom had set in after a few days and we were basically just lying in bed thinking up mischief. Even the Padres were avoiding us, well, Geordie anyway. So we sneaked out of our ward and started playing keepy uppies in the corridor with a severed head we had found. (Not a real one, just exercise, for the use of). By this time Geordie had abandoned the Army issue pyjamas and had gone back to just wearing underpants on his bottom half and a Never Mind The Bollocks T shirt on his top half. We no longer had shrapnel wounds in our asses at this point because they changed the wound every day or so. The trouble was, what he called underpants were grotty yellow Y fronts that were far too big for him (I'm convinced they were someone else's) and they had the unfortunate habit of letting some of his meat and two veg hang out without him realising it. I, as usual, dared not go as far as him, so wore the pyjama bottoms and an Iron Maiden T shirt. Geordie responded to my call of "On the 'ead son" and had lifted the 'football' high with his foot, when the door was opened at the end of the corridor by nurse Churchill. What we didn't know was that on this day she was showing around who, I think, was the CO of the Field

Ambulance unit and someone else with red throat tabs, possibly a Brigadier. As they walked in Geordie had responded to my cries of "on the 'ead son" by shouting "Goooaaaaaalllll!!!!!!" when he and I realised we weren't alone in the corridor. I turned around and saw the brass staring at us. Nurse Churchill looked furious, the CO had his jaw hanging open, and red throat tabs had an expressionless face. We slowly slid to attention, and what a soldierly sight we must have made. When I glanced across to Geordie his cock was hanging out of the side of his grundies...

After what felt like a long time during which red throat tabs scanned us slowly up and down, he said a single word.

"Gunners?"

Geordie did his "Aye sir" and trademark wink at him and I closed my eyes unable to calculate the depth of the shit we were in.

Another hour or so passed and the red throat tabs pointed to some doors next to him and said quietly to Nurse Churchill "Why don't we look in here?"

Shortly after that they split Geordie and me up. Dunno why!

Jonno DP 3RHA

Communing with nature

By 1985 I'd been based in Herford, Germany for a couple of years with 7 Signal Regiment. As frequently happened, we deployed on exercise and I and a colleague were instructed to take our triffid (a radio vehicle consisting of a box body mounted on the back of a Bedford 4 tonner with all manner of radio masts and generators) to a six figure grid reference on the side of a mountain. So far, so normal. Our usual deployment locations were in woods and on high ground because it was better for the radio reception. We arrived in our location about 0200 and put the cam nets up, erected the masts and began communicating as required. Being the Detachment Commander and a kindly soul, I told my crewman to put up his basha and get his head down after we finished, and that I'd wake him when I couldn't stay awake anymore, so off he went.

It was mid-June and the weather was marvellous. Around 0430, dawn began. I turned the interior lights off, opened the back door of the wagon and began to observe God's Big Yellow Lantern as it began to illuminate the landscape. The view was magnificent, I could see for miles. It was absolutely breathtaking.

I hadn't really scanned the map prior to arrival but I began to see that we were just inside the tree line on the forward slope of a small mountain, beneath us, dead ground. 'Dead Ground' for non-military readers is a piece of ground located below the general sweep of the terrain and is of keen interest to the soldier because movement in dead ground cannot be observed.

The sun rose steadily, bathing the scenery in a delicate golden light, treating me to all of this natural beauty and feeding my soul.

I decided that now was a good time to go for a dump. So taking my rifle, webbing, shovel and bog roll, and completely at peace I advanced a few hundred metres down the slope in order to take a crap whilst viewing nature's bounty. Carefully arranging rifle and webbing and sticking my bog roll onto the shovel handle, I adopted the squatting position and commenced, back arched like a Japanese bridge, to snap off a length of dirty spine.

Why is dead ground important to the military map reader? Here's why. As I'm facing downhill, meat and two veg being gently caressed by the morning breeze, I discover that the area to my front is not just dead ground but the very dead ground through which a railway line runs. And it also, at that very moment contained the 05.30 morning commuter train to Hanover.

And yes, some of the passengers even waved...

Sig Tim Knowles, 7 Sigs, Herford.

Tanks very much

It was mid 1991 that I, with the rest of 3RTR, returned from 6 months fun and games in South Armagh.

Taking into account the NI training leading up to the tour we had been off tanks for around a year and the powers that be decided we should all have a Challenger refresher course out on the training area directly behind our camp. One lunch time, Trooper Stu Flackett (loaders side), Lance Corporal McCaffrey (commanding) and myself (driving) jumped in a wagon and off we went for a quick half hour blast around the training area. What could possibly go wrong...

We know the training area very well, having driven around it hundreds of times. There's a lovely fast straight that sweeps in to a 90-degree left hander and the road is flat and really wide so you can take the racing line, even in a Challenger, so we try to touch the apex of the bends. You can just about take it flat out in fourth at around 35 mph but when you're half way round you have to lift off, go down to 3rd gear and power out of the bend.

On the approach, no word of a lie, Flackett says, "Don't lift off! Go flat out, and try to roll it."

Silly! How can we possibly roll 70 tons?! Willing to push the edges, I didn't lift off and the back started to slide out. I applied opposite lock just like you would in a car (pulling the right stick) but the back kept sliding. We hit a four inch kerb perfectly side on, the tracks then dug into the grass verge and that was enough to send the Challenger up and over on to its side. My foot was still flat down on the accelerator, the left track spinning uselessly in the air and the engine revving hard. McCaffrey had wedged himself in

43

the commander's cupola and Flackett was thrown out of the loader's hatch and landed just out of the way. Had it had rolled any further there's a good chance he would have been crushed. The headsets you use inside a tank have a quick release connection for just this sort of incident but it didn't release on Flacketts headset for some reason and his helmet was ripped off his head almost leaving his ears in the headphones.

Flackett then got up, held on to the turret as if to support the tank from toppling further and shouted to McCaffrey to get out. He got out and they then both came around to the front to congratulate me. I was fine, still in the drivers cab. The only damage I sustained was that a bit of brake fluid had leaked on to me as the main brake reservoir is just to the left of the driver.

I switched everything off and clambered out. We all stood back to admire our work and started pissing ourselves laughing. Unfortunately this corner is at a spot that's visible from the whole camp and word soon spread. After a few minutes of us all giggling like school girls Flackett went back to camp to tell the REME they had a recovery job.

Physically we all got away with it, no injuries, but a week or so later I was up in front of the OC and fined a week's wages for damaging army property. Unfortunately, (and he's never let me forget it), McCaffrey was also charged as he was in command. My SSM, Rosie Larcombe was understanding and glad we were all ok, as it could have been very different. He gave me a bit of advice from his years in the job that's stayed with me ever since, "Tanks don't care who they kill."

So that was it. One bright spark took lots of pics with his

flashy camera and sold them round camp. It's his photos you often see on 'Tank mishaps' etc on the internet. They appear every month or so, and I have great pleasure in telling people "Ere, I did that!"

Garry Hodges 3rd Royal Tank Regiment

Ere, Garry Hodges did this!

"Some weren't frightened to go up, some were frightened and couldn't go up. But the brave ones, and I mean the really brave ones, were the ones who were frightened and went up anyway."

Female RAF plotter discussing Battle of Britain pilots.

THAT night in Berlin
(9th November 1989)

I suppose I should start with my wife, Angelica. She is a born and bred Berliner and was telling me the evening before about the rallies held by a million East Germans in their half of the city. There had been a late news article about it on ARD TV the night before which she had seen as she worked in Spandau Hospital.

On the morning of the 9th my day started as normal. I walked to work at Alexander Barracks, arriving around 0815 hours and went straight to the HQ building to check in with the outgoing duty officer, a REME Staff Sergeant coming off his twelve hour duty. The Duty Officer was expected to start at 1800 hours and stay in the duty room, a cramped little box in the cellar of the HQ building which everyone called the bunker, until 0800 hours the following day. I found out that the REME Staff Sergeant had already dropped the folder off into the chief clerk's office and gone to the mess for a nosebag. (Typical pad, getting a free breakfast).

I remember flicking through the duty folder in the chief clerk's office to see the normal one page of events which summed up his stag.

"Nothing out of the ordinary," I thought. Good. A quiet duty tonight would be nice.

I crossed over to my office in the RAOC main stores complex and started my day. It's a funny thing that on that day Werner, my senior civilian supervisor, pointed out we were overdue for a stocktake on the War Reserve Holding we had stored in the basements of RAF Gatow. These had been put there in the early 1960's after the wall had gone up and comprised everything that would be needed to supply us if the Russians decided to attack the West.

After a pretty normal day I left the barracks at 1645 hours to walk home, have a meal and get changed for my duty. At 1745 hours approximately I walked into the HQ building to collect the duty officer's folder and I met our CO, Lieutenant Colonel Frank Steer. We chatted for a few minutes then he left. I picked up the folder and made my way downstairs to the duty officer's bunker.

Everything was as it always was.

As I always did, I checked the contact list was up to date for all REME, RCT and Ordnance Services. There were two telephones in the room. One was for routine calls and the other was only to be used for communications to HQBB (HQ Berlin Brigade) in the Berlin Olympic Stadium, but this one never rang. All fine. I settled down to read my book.

Around 2045 hours I got a phone call from the duty officer at HQBB telling me to contact all the officers commanding the REME, the RCT and our CO. I was to inform them to phone HQBB on the number he had given me. I was then informed that East German authorities were going to open the checkpoints at midnight to allow people from the East to enter West Berlin. If you didn't live through the Cold War I can tell you this was *literally* unbelievable news. The East was very strict on who could and couldn't travel and lots of people had been killed trying to escape to the West.

Astounded though I was I was really happy thinking, if this was true, my wife would get to see the aunties and uncles that she had had no contact with for 28 years. We then got the order to quietly get all military units on standby in case this was a ploy to get Russian and East German troops into West Berlin.

I turned on the radio in the room to listen to the German commentator (I speak fluent German) and was astounded to hear him telling the world that there were over *one million* people at the East/West checkpoints waiting to pass into the West.

Then it started.

At midnight East Berliners came through in their thousands and thousands and then tens of thousands, and West Berliners went out to greet them, many being blood relations. All British military personnel were now on standby in barracks ready to do whatever they were going to be instructed to do. I wish that I had had a TV in that room to see the events unfold.

Then the phone calls started. (Including the phone that never rang from HQ Berlin Brigade.)

The first call made a lot of sense. HQ was asking for 5000 blankets for the Red Cross. In West Berlin the Germans were opening up schools, dance halls, anywhere where they could give East Germans shelter on a cold night. Next was the request to open up our bakery and start baking bread rolls and loaves of bread. This was followed by requests for tea urns and insulated containers so the Red Cross and British Military personnel could dispense hot drinks and soup.

The requests just kept coming, and coming and coming. Camp beds and more blankets. This meant sending our RAOC guys to RAF Gatow to get stocks from the War Reserves stored in the basements. (Werner is not going to be happy, I thought to myself.)

Still the phones rang. This time for RCT buses with drivers to help move families into schools and halls around Berlin.

By 0230 hours we had every department doing something for the assistance of the million plus souls that had walked into West Berlin. Butchers, bakers, dry goods, rations (I thought to myself how would the East Germans get on with their first taste of Compo Sausages and Bacon Grill), general stores, vehicles section. All were struggling to keep up with demand.

Remember I told you about the one page of normal events in the duty officer folder? I was on my second A4 note book by 0300 hours. With the aid of a young Tech Clerk we started to record all items we had released to the German Authorities. Someone, somewhere was going to have to account for, and pay for all this.

My head was hopping and still phones kept ringing asking for more items and contact details of heads of departments. I suppose it was around 0430 hours when one of the lads from the HQ office arrived with some food and a brew. I asked what his job was during this event and he informed me he was the CO's runner. With every military phone going mad in Berlin it was easier to write notes and get the runner to deliver them, so he had just got himself a busy night.

Then the phone calls started to slow down.

The lads in Joint Headquarters and HQBB were starting to realise we just did not have enough stock to handle this scale of events. The French Forces in the north of the city had very limited supplies, the Yanks had as much as us to give, but there comes a time when your stocks are so low you can't give anymore and our chain of supply through the Iron Curtain and up the Berlin corridor was very slow. It was time to start going through every note I had made to make some sense of the stores, vehicles, equipment and food we had issued during the night. The phones were still ringing because the callers could not get through to the department they wanted. The Tech Clerks above me in the offices were working their magic to see what stock we had left on paper while the supply specialists were doing stocktakes in every department and in the war reserves. I remember at one point we were missing two land rovers and a staff car until the paperwork was found later that morning.

At around 0745 hours the chief clerk asked me to divert all phone calls from the duty room to his office. It was time to stand down.

I dragged my exhausted ass up the stairs to the entrance of HQ block and breathed fresh air for the first time in 13 hours. My head was all over the place but I still had to go to my office and get the civilian staff to start checks on all the supplies we had issued.

It was 1100 hours when I finally got home and found my wife crying with joy over this extraordinary night. I sat down in a comfy chair, and whilst telling her the story of my duty, I fell fast asleep.

WO1 SSM G.S. Dymond.

If it doesn't move...

I was awaiting a ship after a course in HMS Vernon in the summer of 1976, remember that summer? If you aren't old enough to, it was a long, long hot one.

One morning we were informed that the next day we were having a 'Royal' visitor, so the establishment had to be swept, tidied and made as presentable as possible. The road from the main gate was a tree lined affair, with the wardroom lawn on the right and a grass verge and football pitch on the left. The wardroom lawn had been getting watered all summer, but the verge on the football pitch side had not, so it was going brown. As we were underemployed, waiting to be sent to a ship, we were told to go to the stores and fetch some green paint and yes, actually told to paint the grass on the verge the same colour as the lawn which we did. With much grumbling and curses about the stupidity of what we were doing, the grass was soon a passable match for the other side of the road and it could please the eye of the royal visitor for the small amount of time it would be visible. It's at times like this you understand why the Russians and the French had revolutions. It didn't last long however, the grass on the verge died and a few months later it ended up having to be tarmacked.

Dinga Bell Royal Navy 1973-1987.

A slight misunderstanding

(Editor's note: To get the full benefit of this story you need to know a few things. Firstly, at this time Northern Ireland was a very conservative place where indelicate things would never be discussed on TV. Secondly, it was a popular myth, started by soldiers, that after a riot where rubber bullets were used, there were none left on the streets, as all the slags had taken them to be used as sex toys. Thirdly, rubber bullets are about six inches long and shaped like a cock. Jonno DP)

When I was the CSM of A Company, The Duke of Edinburgh's Royal Regiment in 1979 we were sent on a six month tour to Northern Ireland. As it was the tenth anniversary of the start of the troubles the OC and myself were asked to go to the Masonic Lodge in Londonderry city centre and give a live lunch time interview on Ulster TV (UTV) to be presented by their reporter Clive Ferguson. It had been a very lively tour up to that point and I think they were looking forward to an exciting interview. There was no messing about with make up or anything like that, we were just sent straight on in full combats.

Ferguson started the interview with, "Now Sergeant Major, you must have some stories to tell!"

"Yes." I said. "I can tell you that only this morning during the search of a lady's house in Londonderry we found, on the mantelpiece, a live rubber bullet."

"It was live, you say!"

"Yes, it certainly was," I confirmed, "and it was painted silver. One of my soldiers noticed that the percussion cap on the base had not been struck."

"I see... is this unusual?"

"Well it is. There are, as I'm sure that you are aware Clive, stories of rubber bullets being put to... well... other uses shall we say."

It was at that point that Ferguson started to look uncertain, the OC next to me remained silent.

I continued. "The lady was told that we would have to take it away, as she could injure herself."

By now Ferguson was shaking his head and mouthing to me "NO!" This interview remember, is being broadcast live.

I carried on. "The lady said to us 'I don't know what I'll do without it, I use it every day.'"

An ashen faced Ferguson was by now wide eyed, waving his arms around and frantically mouthing "NO! NO! NO! NO!"

I waited a suitable time, which must have seemed an age to Ferguson and then said, "She told us that she used it to hit her Hoover to make it go when she turned it on."

There was visible relief from Ferguson, and when we finished he wasn't even angry, (I don't think he realised I was doing it on purpose), he was just grateful that his job hadn't ended along with the interview.

Just another day in the life of a British soldier.

Note: The OC in this story was Major Stephen Saunders, a fine officer who went on to command the Battalion and reached the rank of Brigadier. In 2000 whilst posted to Athens as the British Military Attaché he was ambushed and murdered at traffic lights by assassins on a motor cycle. Although those responsible were caught and sentenced, there is no doubt that the Duke of Edinburgh's Royal Regiment that day lost an officer of the highest calibre, with all the qualities and attributes that one expects from the Infantry of the British Army.

CSM D Wiggins, A Company, The Duke of Edinburgh's Royal Regiment

Just in case it should be of interest to any ladies reading this (well, I guess any blokes too) I discovered, whilst researching some details of this story, that you can buy these rubber bullets on ebay. I shit you not. Erm... enjoy! Jonno DP.

L2A2 British Army Rubber Bullet. (Picture courtesy of eBay – seriously.)

Who has the cleverest officers?

Once, while I was a commander of a FRT half-track we were tasked to put on a demonstration of an auxiliary generator change on a centurion tank near Sandhurst for several large groups of NATO officers. The Sandhurst Staff College took advantage of the proximity of this large event and brought along some potential Rodneys training there at the time. Before it started a Major from Sandhurst gave us a briefing on what to expect. He was a nice guy, not stuffy at all and he showed me a chart which showed the average exam results that a Student Officer needed to get into the various Regiments and Corps. I noticed that REME officers were at the bottom of the list. Surprised, I questioned this. His answer was a classic. He said, you REME chaps are a bright lot, you don't need intelligent officers. True.

Ron Allen REME

Maybe we should have TOGed harder

T'was the early hours on the 20th of November. For those of you who are not familiar with that date it is the anniversary of the Battle of Cambrai, the main battle honour of the Royal Tank Regiments (RTR) when in 1917 the first large scale, effective use of tanks in warfare happened. For a young trooper soon to be promoted to Lance Corporal, (that soon changed), it was an eventful date in the year with many an alcoholic beverage consumed.

It was 1996, and I was in 1RTR, stationed in Aliwal barracks, Tidworth. For the units that shared the same barracks with us Cambrai Day was an absolute nightmare with paintings, Land rovers and orderly officers going missing. (Normally found several days later chained to a radiator with no food or water, and that was just the Land Rovers.) In a previous year a horse had also been stolen and some bright spark decided to paint it. It didn't survive. On this fateful Cambrai night me and my sidekick Dicko decided that it was all very well getting up to this stuff, but we were wanting bigger fish to fry. So fairly intoxicated we roamed the camp looking for the Holy Grail of mischief. It wasn't long before we found what we were looking for. The ultimate wanking material for a Gunnery instructor, the TOGS trailer, sat on its lonesome in dark shadows waiting to be released. The TOGs trailer was a big and expensive piece of kit. It carried a Thermal Observation Gunnery Sight and was used so the gunnery instructors could see what was happening in the turret whilst we were live firing on the tank ranges.

Now in theory it sounds like a piece of piss. Two highly motivated roughty toughty soldiers take the TOGS trailer from its current location, leave it on the regimental square and go off laughing. But alas, there were certain factors that were against us:

1. We were pissed.
2. There was a steep fuck off hill we needed to take it down.
3. The Orderly Officer would be hot on our heels, ready to kill us if we got him out of his wanking chariot.
4. We could barely see or communicate with each other due to alcohol and tears of laughter.

In spite of the meticulous and detailed planning described above things started to go a bit pear shaped as soon as we released the handbrake. It didn't take long before the TOGS trailer picked up a fair bit of speed with us hanging on to the back. At this stage we were just laughing thinking 'Well, this is easy! It's almost as if the trailer has a mind of its own and is helping us!' Then it began picking up a bit more speed. Then a bit more. Then even more... Before long we were both sprinting like we could hear a PTI shouting out 1022.....1024.... As I looked across at Dicko his legs were nothing but a blur, and I was struggling to keep up.

Then it happened.

We both (now for the purposes of the story try and picture this in slow motion), looked at each other and cried out "NOOOOOOO!!!!" as we released our grip on the TOGS trailer. We watched helplessly as it started to gain more and more momentum as it hurtled down the hill. To the side of the trailer's path was a car park packed with a lot of very new, very shiny tax free cars that the lads had bought just before the regiment left Germany. But this was so far off the direction of travel the trailer was taking that there was no way it could possibly smash into it..........
could it?

There was no stopping this TOGS trailer now. It was moving like it was possessed by the devil, and I swear I heard it giggle as it swerved and headed straight for the car park, delighted at the carnage that was to follow. For what seemed like an eternity Dicko and I watched in horror until the TOGS trailer hit the embankment just before the car park. The embankment was perfectly shaped to act like a launch pad for the trailer so it could fly gracefully into the middle of densely packed and expensive German engineering. By this time I had stopped running and had closed my eyes waiting to hear the crash of metal on metal that would wake the entire camp in one go.

By a miracle it never happened.

The Satan trailer came to a teetering halt finely balancing itself on top of the embankment, swinging gently to and fro. Again, I swear I could hear it. It was quietly weeping because it had not reached its chosen destination.

In contrast with the clarity with which I remember the events above, the next couple of hours are a blur. Running from the Orderly Officer, dodging the gate guard and hiding under my bed until I was found by the Provo whereupon I was escorted quick time to the pokey to be reunited with Dicko. We both never got promoted that year.

Trooper (Yes, Trooper) Donaldson 1RTR.

The 'Dance of the flaming arseholes' #1

In 1965 I was part of a REME Inspection team doing an RHA regiment at Hildesheim. We didn't know what options there were for entertainment in the evening, so a resident REME guy Corporal W. suggested there might be a show at the NAAFI and we should go there first.

We went inside the crowded NAAFI and realised it was getting louder and more crowded as time went on. Then we heard sudden a roar as a naked trooper jumped onto a table, stuck a rolled-up newspaper up his arse, lit it, and started singing Zulu Warrior. I think the idea was to finish the song before the flames reach the tender parts. In this case he was successful and his reward was everybody nearby threw their beer at him to put out the fire. Oh to have had a video camera back then. At closing time my mate got into a fight, as you do. After a bit I thought I had best separate them and as I pulled him away I distinctly heard a loud crack. He didn't say anything or do anything so I thought that maybe I had imagined it. Off he went in the direction of his block. The next day I found he had a broken collar bone. That beer made you stronger than you think!

Derek Grater REME

"You see lads, it's all a question of mind over matter. We don't mind, and you don't matter."

My troop Sergeant in basic training, and ten thousand others.

Swapsies?

Whilst I was in Northern Ireland I got quite pally with some of the lads in the Ulster Defence Regiment. I would often sit with them drinking their home made alcoholic potato juice which was called Poitín (pronounced 'Pusheen').
One day on patrol I was admiring one of the UDR lads G3 rifle and I thought that looks really ally, so I asked him if he fancied swapping his G3 for my SA80 for a bit as we were only on a short patrol. He was fine with it and said, "Yeah, no problem." I had no training on this weapon whatsoever, but as I was only eighteen years old I felt it looked pretty cool, which is the main thing when you are eighteen.
Halfway through the patrol something happened and we got split up. He jumped on a helicopter and got lifted out, going fuck knows where. So now I'm stood there in the middle of the Ulu watching the weapon that I signed for disappearing over the horizon along with my chances of staying in the army, and I'm shitting myself.
I went into my brick commander and said, "Excuse me corporal, I need to speak to the sergeant, I've got a bit of a problem."
He asked me what the problem was and I held up the G3 and said, "This".
He was really mellow and didn't go off on one or anything. He just sighed and said, "Riiiiiiiiiiight."
All too soon the patrol was over and we entered the camp. By now my rusty Sheriff's badge is twitching as I'm thinking about what the hell I am going to say in my defence. If you have never served, losing your weapon, which I effectively had, is about as serious a fuckup as you can make. But the Lord God himself must have smiled on

me. Standing inside the camp gates was the UDR man with a big grin on his face holding my SA80. He just said, "Shall we swap back now?"

Simon (Trooper) Pickford. 1st Battalion Royal Green Jackets.

Things you thought you knew #2.

There was never a nuclear near miss.

Lieutenant Colonel Stanislav Petrov. The man who saved the world.

I am a former British Soldier and very patriotic, but I genuinely believe every city in the world should have a statue of former Lieutenant Colonel Stanislav Petrov of the Soviet Air Defence Forces. And every 26th of September flowers should be laid at the feet of them in gratitude. He probably saved your life, mine, and possibly the entire planet from becoming a lifeless lump of rock.

In the early hours of the morning of the 26th September 1983 the Soviet Union's early-warning systems detected incoming missiles from the United States. Colonel Petrovs job was to register enemy missile launches and inform his superiors. All of the data he had in front of him pointed to this being a genuine launch and not a false alarm. The Soviet doctrine was for them to immediately launch their own missiles in retaliation before the US strike destroyed their ground based ICBMs. The estimated flight time before the impact of the American missiles was mere minutes and Stanislav had to make a decision, and he had to make it now, now, now!

His choices were to report it as an attack, which would certainly have resulted in Soviet missiles being launched, or report it to his superiors and let them have the responsibility. This would also have resulted in a Soviet launch. Had he chosen either of these two options it is almost certain that no one would have stopped it, or even questioned it.

He later said to an interviewer he froze in place when he first saw and heard the alarms.

"The siren howled, but I just sat there for a few seconds, staring at the big, back-lit, red screen with the word 'Launch' on it."

His systems were telling him that the reliability of the alert was rated 'Highest'. There was absolutely no reason to doubt it. America had launched a nuclear missile at Russia. About a minute later he received another alert. Another missile had been launched. Then a third, then a fourth, then a fifth, then a sixth. Stanislavs computers changed their readouts from 'Alert' to 'Missile Strike'.

Decades after the event Stanislav told interviewers that he felt like he was sitting on a hot frying pan, but he couldn't move. There was no hard and fast rule on how long he was allowed to think, but obviously the longer he waited the worse position his country would be in to retaliate. Asked decades later why he made the decision he made, he said to journalists that he had two competing arguments in his mind at the time.

On the one hand he knew that the alert was almost certainly correct, even though the Soviet satellite controllers told him there were no launches. They could have been deceived by American interference, have malfunctioned, or simply have made a mistake. And in any case, they were just backups, Stanislav's system was the main one. And his detection system was brand new, the state of the Soviet art...

On the other hand, it was odd that the satellites had nothing. And why had the Americans only launched five missiles? It seemed an odd way to start a nuclear attack. Why not, as the Soviet planners said it would be, an all-out attack with everything the USA had? He knew that with the prevailing frosty relations between East and West in 1983, retaliation from the Soviet Union would have been certain. Only three weeks earlier the USSR had shot down Korean airlines flight 007 killing everyone on board and the Cold War had never been colder. And odd again that his system reported that the probability of the report was so high, and other systems reported zero activity. And maybe the new system had bugs...

The standing orders stated clearly that the decision was to be based on his computer. The others were only advisory. He was the duty officer.

The decision rested with him.

He made his decision.

He picked up the phone and committed what was officially a breach of his instructions and a dereliction of duty.

He contacted the duty officer in the Soviet army's headquarters and reported a system malfunction. If he was wrong the detonation of impacting missiles would have started a few minutes later.

He later said that after about twenty minutes of talking on the phone and checking his systems he realised he had heard and felt no nuclear explosions. He described it as 'such a relief'.

Talking about it decades later he said that he thought the odds of it being genuine were about 50:50 and his decision could quite easily have gone the other way. A factor may have been that he was the only officer in his team who had received a civilian education. All the other officers had had a military education and were much more likely to automatically obey orders, whatever they were, without thinking about it first.

A few days later he received an official reprimand for not filing his paperwork correctly that night. His standing instructions were that he should write them down as they happened.

When he was chastised for this he allegedly replied "I had a phone in one hand and the intercom in the other, and I don't have a third hand". (I bet that went down a treat!)

Let's stop and think about this for a minute. He was the single step, the one person who stopped accidental nuclear Armageddon, something that would probably have destroyed the entire human race, and he received an official reprimand for his paperwork.

I find it a strange comfort that the Red Army reacted in the same mindless way that I would expect of the British Army. "Yes, yes, I *know* you stopped the entire human race being wiped out, but we can't have people disobeying orders can we?"

And I can hear myself saying "Well, I see your point sir, but doesn't saving the entire planet give me just a *little* credit?"

Later investigations showed that the false alarm was caused by the unusual alignment of sunlight on high altitude clouds above the American state of North Dakota and the orbits of certain satellites. Although he did receive praise for his handling of the incident from General Yury

Votintsev, then commander of the Soviet Air Defence's Missile Units, (and the first to reveal the incident to the public in the 1990s), he was intensively interrogated by his superiors and they continually questioned his judgement. Apart for the bollocking for not filing his paperwork correctly he received no further official punishment or praise. Petrov said in later interviews that to praise or reward him would embarrass his superiors and the designers of the missile detection system, and it would mean that they would have to be punished.

Shortly after he saved mankind he was reassigned to a less sensitive post. He took early retirement from the military but denied he had been forced out, as has been claimed in some western news agencies, and went to work at the research institute that had developed the early warning system. This is a job interview I would have liked to have seen.

After the story came out Petrov received many awards from various organisations for what he had done, particularly in America, but in 1998 he suffered from a mental breakdown and is quoted as saying, "I was made a scapegoat."

In 2013 a feature-length Danish documentary about the incident called The Man Who Saved the World was made by Peter Anthony and received generally favourable reviews.

Petrov lived in his house near Moscow until his death on the 19th of May 2017 from hypostatic pneumonia. I think we should leave the last words to the man himself.

"My late wife for 10 years knew nothing about it. 'So what did you do?' she asked me. 'Nothing. I did nothing.'"

Researched and written by Jonno DP.

"At some point you will leave the military, but the military will not leave you."

Anon

It does what it says on the tin

I was a Petty Officer in the Royal Navy stationed at RNAS Culdrose up until 2012. In the winter of 2010 one of the station duties was as part of the on call 'Snow & Ice' team which was led by the Aircraft Salvage (crash 'n smash) Department.

Unusually, it had snowed rather heavily over the New Year and into the January while most of the station were away on Christmas leave. I remember this rather well as it was my birthday over the break and on that particular day I was stuck on camp whilst my wife was at home seven miles away in front of a roaring fire.

I wasn't happy about this at all, but at least I got to zoom around a closed airfield in a Land Rover doing doughnuts and generally having a ball doing dangerous shit whilst no one was watching!

At the time RNAS Culdrose had a requirement to provide the Search and Rescue cover for the South West and the Scilly Isles. One aircraft was ready to go at a moment's notice and a second aircraft was ready to go 45 minutes after the first.

However, the usually reliable weather forecast had not been accurate and an unexpectedly heavy dump of snow had arrived overnight. Ice and snow on a runway cause obvious problems and it HAD to be cleared. The navy had de-icing fluid which was usually available to our section which would have been great, but in good old MoD fashion it had been withdrawn only weeks previously. (Yes, over Christmas, cos it never snows then right?)

The Squadron had sensibly put the two alert aircraft in the hangar overnight, but now could not get them out again because the hard standing and taxiway were covered in

70

snow. Initially the snow ploughs were brought in to clear it, but it left hard packed icy snow on the concrete and tarmac.

Hmmm…

The only other thing we had was an ANTI-icing fluid. The instructions written on it were explicit. DO NOT put on an already iced surface as the fluid will freeze.

Had we swept and shovelled the snow there and then it would have taken a while, but we could have done it, few as we were. But as it happened the duty senior officer was Commander Air. He told us to get de-icing fluid out of storage and spray it on. He was informed of its withdrawal and replacement with the *anti*-icing fluid, and he was also advised that the instructions specifically said not to apply it to an already frozen surface. With the daring and brilliance that marks out officers from us ordinary mortals he instructed us to spray it on anyway. We advised him against it, reminding him of the instructions on the tin, but he was adamant that we were to spray it on, so we did.

Within an hour or so the aircraft hardstandings and roadways were frozen solid. They were almost perfectly smooth, almost smooth enough to ice skate on, and this is a really big area. Ahh well. That's life in a blue suit. So the senior officer comes out, inspects his new ice rink and orders us to lift it. I am sure the phrase "You told us to spray it when we warned you not to… why don't you bloody lift it?" popped into more than one mind.

So now we have another issue. How to lift this thick ice.

The snowploughs couldn't get rid of it. They'd tried.

The runway sweepers couldn't lift it. They'd tried.

The answer? Yes, you guessed correctly! Us. Shovels and brooms. Chipping and sweeping. In sub-zero temperatures.

Now as a duty section we did not have the manpower to 'efficiently' clear the newly laid ice, so we passed it back up the chain of command. The only pool of manpower available was a class of trainee Aircraft Handlers (Chockheads) from the training school on the station. These poor Jacks and Jennies were mustered at the Squadron and given their chilly task, twenty minutes on, twenty minutes off. It really was bitterly cold so we went to the stores to get some cold weather clothing. Guess what? We didn't have any of that kit either. Doesn't it make you proud to belong to one of the premier military forces in the world? The one that withdraws de-icer in December and doesn't have any cold weather kit in the stores when snow is falling?

It must have taken them about three hours of slippery, freezing muscle wrenching graft in total to clear that ice. All because of a senior officer who didn't believe what it said on the tin!!

Adrian Eason Basset. Royal Navy.

It's a dog's life

Back in the early nineties I was a Corporal at 4 Armoured REME Workshops in Detmold and was detached for a few months to 14 Sigs in Osnabruck. I was sharing a room with another REME VM whom I will call Pete. Of course, and as per usual, no pets were allowed in barracks.

One morning I was at brekky and Pete joined me a few minutes after I arrived. Pete and I were discussing the usual, birds and beer, when we noticed the Sigs RP Sergeant loitering and earwigging our conversation. I decided I would give him something to listen to as he was a nosy twat.

I said to Pete, "Is the dog ok? I didn't see him this morning after his walk and going to do his business. Did you shut the window before you came across to the canteen?" Pete, being of the same mindset as me, immediately caught on and replied, "I thought you had!"

The conversation then went on to whose turn it had been to walk and pee the dog, who was last out of the room and who should have ensured the window was closed. Like an old married couple, we were quietly bickering about who fed him last, walked him last and whose turn it was to take him for the weekend etc. All the while the RP Sgt was earwigging nearby and trying to maintain the nonchalant expression on his face! After a few minutes he decided that he had heard enough and butted in demanding to be told about the dog, what the feck it was doing in our accommodation, and how long we had had it. He also wanted to know the type of dog it was and where it was if not in our room. Both of us again blamed each other for its escape and gave a description to the RP

Sergeant who radioed the guardroom and got the guard and duty RP's out to search the camp for our beloved pet. He then left with the parting words accompanied by a jabbing finger, "YOU are deep in the shit and the RSM will be informed".

As soon as he was out of sight Pete and I pissed ourselves laughing! We finished scoff and went to the LAD and started work. Just before NAAFI break we were summoned to the ASMs office. When we arrived he wanted to know what the hell was going on as the RSM had called him about two of his VMs having a dog in the accommodation and that the guard were still out looking for it! Desperately trying not to giggle, I explained the situation to him and he 'suggested' we trot along to see the RSM which we did.

After tick tocking into the RSM's office and after the screaming had ceased, I told him what had happened and why we led the nosy RP Sergeant along. Fair play to him, he was old school and saw the funny side and sent us away back to the ASM after calling the guardroom to say the dog had been located!

I got a flea in my ear from the ASM, again a decent spud, but the RP Sergeant checked our room for days after In the hope he would catch us with our pooch and nail us for fecking his guard about!

Cpl John Cox, 4 Armoured REME Workshop Detmold

The Karate kid

Ginge was a lad from my unit in Bracht and one day he decided to go into the music cafe in town on his own. He was in there for a bit minding his own business when five lads of Turkish extraction decided they wanted to fuck the Englander about and started chucking insults his way. Ginge grew up in Moss Side, Manchester, so five on one wasn't a problem to him. After a few minutes he was fed up with their bullshit and pointed to them in turn saying "You, you, you, you and you, fucking outside now!" Ginge stepped outside, shook his shoulders down, kicked off his shoes and went into a karate stance. The Turks wisely decided they didn't want any of this mad squaddie, so they made their apologies and went back into the bar. Ginge put his shoes on, walked back in himself, picked up his beer and carried on drinking as if nothing had happened. The next morning at work Ginge regaled us with his story of bluff, not missing out how glad he was it had worked as Turks regularly carried knives, and were not afraid to use them.

About a week later myself and my roommate Mark had been drinking in a few bars in Kaldenkirchen, on the Dutch German border. Mark was a great bloke, sadly no longer with us, a real character. Once when I was duty Dogs driver he asked if he could borrow my bomber jacket to go down town in. After I finished the duty I went back to the block to get some sleep. About an hour later I was woken up by a scraping noise and flashing lights. Mark had bought back a 6 foot long 'Road closed' barrier that had the flashing lights still going on it. Traffic cones are one thing, but for fuck's sake! Later that day I picked up the jacket that I had loaned him, which he had left on the sideboard. It felt very heavy, so I went through the pockets, they were full of turnips. Baffled, swearing, and picking the mud out I asked him why. He had no idea, but it wasn't unusual to wake up after a heavy night's drinking to find something unusual in the room.

Anyway, back to the night in Kaldenkirchen. Totally paralytic, we sat waiting at a bus stop after being fucked off repeatedly by the local taxi drivers. Whilst sat there we were approached by a group of pissed up, rowdy Germans and the normal verbal engagement began. Having had enough of the group I decided to do the same bluff as Ginge had done to the Turks. "Watch this mate, they will piss themselves and run."

I stood up from the bench in the bus shelter, and, as you've probably guessed, went into the karate stance, "**Hiiiiii..ya!!**" I shouted and waited for the Germans to run away.

Something was wrong, I was lying on my back in a bush. Fuck me, I thought, I must be well pissed.

I got myself up and again went back into the karate stance, "**Hiiiiii..ya!!**"

Again, I was back in the bush.

Mark was in hysterics, he was laughing so much he had fallen off the bench.

Again I stood up.

Again, I went into the karate stance, but I didn't even get as far as the 'Hiiiiya' this time.

I saw the leg come round, but being too pissed and too slow I ended up back in the bush.

I was lying there having a think when I noticed the German Civil Police had turned up and were arresting Mark, who was still pissing himself laughing. I stood up for the umpteenth time and saw that even sat in the police car he was still laughing. The German who had been fighting with me, or rather, who was rearranging the hedge with me, was talking to the policeman. He was good about it to be fair, he managed to persuade the cop that we were all friends just having fun and got him to release Mark. When the GCP left the German spoke to me. "You Englanders, up, down, up, down. Why do you never give up?" He slapped me on the back and said "Come, we go for a beer." So myself and Mark ended up in yet another bar, this time drinking with our new German friends. It turns out the bush rearranger was the German under 21 National Karate champion, and we had a fantastic time in the bar with them.

Spike Elliott MT/MHE Bracht 1987-1990

Editor's note. If you read volume 1 of We Were Cold Warriors there were several great tales signed off as "Mark RAOC Bracht". The Mark mentioned in Spike's stories above are the same guy. Sadly, Mark passed away recently, so RIP mate from Spike and me, and thanks for all the laughs.

A sobering experience

Back when I joined in 1984 the WRAC were a separate corps to the rest of the army, but several trades were open to us. Basic training, all six weeks of it, was in Guildford and after the passing out parade we were dispersed to the training regiments for whichever Corps was lucky enough to be getting us. Consequently I spent a few months at 8 Sigs in Catterick training to be a Data Telegraphist (DTG) before being sent to my first posting at 16 Signal Regiment in Krefeld. The regiment consisted of HQ squadron (as usual this was all the admin, Catering Corps etc) and then four squadrons. 1 Squadron was located in JHQ Rheindahlen, 4 Squadron was at 1 BR Corps in Bielefeld, and 2 and 3 squadrons were in Krefeld. I was in 3 squadron which had F(oxtrot) troop and J(uliet) troop. I was in F Troop who, naturally, considered themselves the coolest troop in all creation.

We had a Lieutenant as the troop OC and he was supported by a Staff Sergeant and a Sergeant. There were various Corporals and Lance Corporals and a whole bunch of Signalmen and Privates. Only one of the NCOs at that time was a woman. 16 Sigs' job was to provide communications for various organisations in time of war but not much else. 1 and 4 Squadrons actually had 'proper' jobs at the Comcen and switchboards. But 2 and 3 squadrons were there for the war and consequently, as with most other regiments in BAOR at the time, were in a constant state of 'hurry up and wait' for that war. Most of the time we were in barracks getting ready for the next exercise or recovering from the last. The word was that the CO didn't really want women, but back then the WRAC were making a case for women being integrated into as many of the trades as possible and showing that we were as good as the men, while having to wear our own cap-badges and only being attached to the regiments we were posted to. Consequently there were only ever around 25 women at the regiment at any one time although 1 and 4 squadrons were mostly women.

This meant a lot of painting our wagons two thirds green, one third black with the occasional foray, depending on the prevailing attitude of the troop OC, into painting the wheel nuts and Vauxhall logo on the front of the wagon red. And then painting them green or black again when someone pointed out that red wheel nuts weren't really camouflaged. Some of those trucks had layers and layers of paint on them because we didn't have the facilities to give them a proper wash after an exercise, so we brushed off the worst of the mud and painted what couldn't be removed.

It wasn't all exercise and exercise preparation though; every day we had to start the wagons and check they were in working order. Occasionally I'd be allowed to drive it once around the wagon park but only when nobody was looking. Starting the engine in winter using the cold-start capsules was always fun, like a bunch of glue sniffers! Mostly, though, we spent weeks on end sweeping leaves, painting trucks, sweeping leaves and for the WRAC a very special treat: there was a (male) toilet block outside our troop. It was a disgusting, vile, stinking cesspit that we were ordered to clean, and of course, we couldn't complain because that kind of resistance was always greeted with extras and cries of "The girls can't hack it, we knew it".

One thing we did regularly were SOP kit inspections. We lugged our SOP kit to the troop, formed up with plenty of space between us, and laid it all out in the prescribed manner. Often the inspection was the troop Staff Sergeant or Sergeant having a quick look over everyone's kit to make sure we had it all, and then telling us to pack it all away. But occasionally they got some kind of cob on about women in the army and we were given extras for not having feminine hygiene products in our packs. This was mostly pointless, because if we ever did go on exercise with a box of tampons the guys usually found them and wore the 'white mice' as earrings.

Occasionally we'd have weapons training. We'd be called out to the front of the troop and told to form up with something like, "Women on the left – draw an SMG. Men on the right – draw an SLR. WAIT! Where are you going private xxxxxxxx? F Tribe form up on the other side of the girls, grab a spear and a shield".

Yes, we had 4 black signalmen in our troop and they had to put up with this kind of thing on a daily basis. But it was all 'bantz and fun' back then.

I was allocated to a small detachment within the troop consisting of a Land Rover towing a generator, a radio relay wagon and a three ton box-bodied wagon which housed our communications equipment. There were usually around ten personnel consisting of a DTG corporal, a tech Corporal, a couple of lineys and the rest were Lance Corporals or signalmen. Then there was me, and usually two, but sometimes only one other WRAC – we weren't allowed to go on exercise individually without a chaperone!

One February it was absolutely freezing. Real brass monkey weather. Active edge was called early in the morning and we formed up in our wagons on the square ready to defend the homeland. Or something. As usual there were a few hours of hurry up and wait during which we got colder and colder. It started to snow big fat flakes and the sky was dark grey before lunchtime when we eventually got underway. And so began, possibly, the coldest week of my life and I've been in Russia in winter. To this day I swear I couldn't feel my feet from the time we bugged out until about 2 days after we got back. Our little convoy peeled off towards wherever it was we were going, and after a few hours we arrived in a small wooded area on the edge of some farmland. We set up our equipment and the guys all unpacked their flowery duvets and extra pillows. For this exercise, Wintex, there was only me and one other WRAC. We watched in increasing disbelief as the guys brought out camp-beds and even a space heater. It was our first exercise and of course our team hadn't advised us to secrete anything like this in the wagon over the weeks before the exercise. We also discovered they were all wearing army issue thermal underwear and had lovely thick leather NI gloves. We had nothing like that, just the regular WRAC No. 2 uniform gloves, rather elegant black leather things completely useless to keep your hands warm. There had been no issuing of WRAC thermal long-johns prior to the exercise. We learned later that there were indeed such items but they were all at some depot in the UK and treated as non-urgent because 'The girls don't go out in the field'. Eventually some tent poles and a 9 by 9 tent appeared at our feet.

"We brought you this." said the detachment commander cheerily, "Don't worry, we'll help you put it up".

As it turned out we had to stand and watch because our hands were so cold. Unlike the men we had no camp beds and were expected to unroll our sleeping bags directly onto the snow.

In the end the pair of us decided that we'd sleep in the Land Rover and do the cooking and whatever in the tent. After the exercise was over our troop Sergeant actually tore a strip off our detachment commander for not giving us any advice beyond 'wear tights under your combats' for our first exercise. We were wiser for subsequent exercises though.

I'm not actually sure what the game-plan was, but we spent the best part of a week parked up in that corner. It was quite nice at times, although it was around -13°C during the day and a lot colder at night. One of the problems of being a small detachment with old equipment was that fairly often our radio signal would drop out. Our Corporal would jump in the Land Rover and zoom off to the nearest telephone box. In those days they were yellow and were commonly called a 'Yellow Comcen' by us as the relay dropped out so often. During the day this little trip was no problem, but during the night when my fellow WRAC and I were sleeping in the back of the vehicle it got rather uncomfortable. Due to the large amount of noise a Land Rover makes it wasn't noticed by the driver that we were being thrown about the back, zipped into our 'green maggot' sleeping bags and completely unable to free ourselves.

One afternoon it was so cold our faces hurt but we couldn't all hang about in the back of the box-bodied truck, we had to mount guards etc. One mid-afternoon when we were on stag our troop sergeant turned up to see how we were.

"Look," he said, "I know this isn't really allowed but there's no harm in it, plus it's good for morale and it is fucking freezing." With that he pulled out a bottle of rum, and dolloped a generous slug in the mugs that had magically appeared in our outstretched hands.

"Cheers!" he said.

"Cheers!" we chorused in reply.

He warned us not to breathe a word, hopped back into his vehicle and with a wave of his hand he was off. We nodded and waved back.

Ten minutes later our troop staff sergeant appeared. "Everyone OK? Food OK? Mail getting through?" he chuckled at his WW2 style joke, and carried on. "So, this hasn't been official for several years but what the heck, it's brass monkey weather and if you don't tell anyone I won't." We were ready with our mugs for a hefty measure of rum and it was "Cheers" and "Chin chin" all round. We were feeling warm and fuzzy when he left and decided a round of tea was in order. We'd no sooner brewed up when up zoomed our squadron OC. He didn't faff about. "Oi, you lot! Rum ration!" By the time he left we'd had 2 rounds of drinks from him and we were ready to party. And that is when the tech corporal remembered the two orange handbags (Ten packs of Herforder Pilsner, a truly disgusting beer that only squaddies drank) he'd stowed in the side lockers. Happy days!

Anon

The night river crossing

We were on a training exercise down in Brecon for a couple of weeks back in 1992 and one particular night exercise included a river crossing. Now as you may know the temperatures down there in Wales can change really fast. One hour sunshine, the next rain. Thunder to hail, frost and snow in no time! I had my fair share experiencing the weather down there I can tell ya...

We were on the night river crossing exercise, probably about 2 in the morning. The sky was clear, frost had settled, and it was pretty nippy. But more worryingly, our boss (the Platoon Lieutenant) was leading the way. He was taking us through hedges, up and down every incline he could find, along ridges, finally arriving at the river. (If you don't know, young officer's map reading skills leave a lot to be desired.)

I will always remember the boss halting the patrol with his hand signals making a silhouette like a tree (I could see him clearly as I was the forward section radio operator). We adopted the usual kneeling position with the rest of the section in all round defence. He whipped his red-light and map out and started his usual rustling which was audible from a couple of hundred yards away. He turned and spoke to the platoon sergeant in a low whisper saying, "Right. We'll cross here and form up on the other side."

I heard the sarge saying, "Uhhh....ohhkkaaay."

"Is there a problem?"

Still whispering, the sarge said "I think we should go further along, its looking a bit deep here don't you think?"

To be honest it did look deep. And you could see the speed the water was doing as it broke and foamed over some rocks.

The boss replied, "Naaah it's fine, we'll cross here."

"Okay!" said the sarge calmly, sounding like he knew what was going to happen.

The boss gave the whispered order "Prepare to move" and you could hear the whispering echo "Prepare to move" being relayed down the line.

I was about a metre away from the boss, I can see him now, silhouetted heroically against the night sky, moving decisively to lead his men. As if in slow motion he stepped into the river, but instead of finding something solid his foot kept sinking into the river.

He disappeared with a loud splash, followed by a quiet gurgle.

Bear in mind he was fully kitted up with his lid, gat, full webbing and bergen. That's a lot of weight! After a bit he bobbed to the surface and said "FUCK!" But credit where it's due, he did it in a whisper, which is impressive as he must have lost his bollocks in that freezing river.

Laughing tactically (in other words quietly) was a mission in itself!

The sarge reached in, grabbed the boss, and was straining to pull him out of the water onto the bank, fighting against the extra weight of water in his kit and the fast river current trying to pull him back in. The boss was splashing everywhere, trying to get out, desperate to escape that icy river... In the end he was dragged out and he flopped onto the bank like a pile of wet rags. I suppose the only positive thing was that, like all of us, the kit in his bergen was wrapped inside waterproof bags.

After a bit the boss stood up, started shaking himself and swearing quietly. When he was done, the sarge, all Zen like, cool, calm and collected turned to the lads and quietly whispered, "Right. Follow me."

We walked about 20 metres down river to a wide shallow area and crossed. The water was shin height and we got no more than wet feet. We formed the other side of the river, and with the boss squelching in front of us we moved into a nearby copse. We could have followed him even if we couldn't see him. His teeth were chattering like a runaway gimpy.

Happy days!

Jason Strange 1 RWF

Just do the right thing!

One day I was in a brick patrolling near Newtown Hamilton, Northern Ireland. We had the brief to knock on doors and be friendly with the locals and check that everything was ok, but also to see if we could pick up any useful intelligence. We had been out for two or three days sleeping in gorse bushes and things like that, so we were tired, grotty and hungry. We found that for some strange reason, when we knocked on doors the local civilians weren't keen to talk to a group of filthy, heavily armed infantrymen!

So we get to this farm and the patrol commander calls me across, reminds me of the brief, and tells me I am to knock on the door. I asked why me, and he said because I was by far the youngest, (I was just 18) and I would look less threatening to the occupants and therefore they would be more likely to talk.

"What do I say?" I said.

"Just be nice. Put them at ease." he replied impatiently, looking at his map.

"But what do I do if..."

"Just fucking do it," he snarled, "do what you think is right, keep 'em happy."

Feeling way out of my depth I knocked on the door. A couple of the lads were visible, putting on their friendliest fake smiles. The rest were invisible, around the perimeter. The door was answered by a lady who called her husband to the door, while she went back to the kitchen. Their name was King I remember. So I am there chatting away and it turns out the family consists of the farmer, his wife and his daughter, but his daughter was not in the house. I asked the father where she was and he said she was away in England studying at Manchester University. I told the farmer that I was from Manchester and he called his wife back, "Hey Betty, hey Betty, this bloke's from Manchester. His missus came back and said, "You look sound, come on in in."

I didn't really know what to do for the best but remembering the instructions to 'keep 'em happy' I went in, unloading my rifle and pocketing the magazine. The wife asked me if I wanted a cup of tea.

"Yes please!"

"Would you like some biscuits?"

"Ooohh, yes please!"

She insisted I sit down on the comfiest chair in the room right next to a roaring fire and started chatting away to me. I'm thinking this is great! Well I'm sat there having a lovely time, eating all the biscuits and the wife is asking me all about Manchester, what it's like, and how was it for me growing up there, my school etc. I was on my second slice of cake when I noticed my patrol commander walk past the window for the third time. This time though, he stopped, shaded his eyes and pressed his nose against the window. He turned away and stopped dead in his tracks, turned back, shaded his eyes and looked in again, straight at me. I waved.

He didn't wave back.

Moments later there was a knock at the door and the lady of the house excused herself to answer it. I couldn't hear what my patrol commander said, but it did sound like he was talking through clenched teeth. It was drizzling outside. The lady apologised for forgetting everyone left outside and asked if he and all the lads wanted a nice cup of tea. Unable to resist the temptation he accepted. She shut the door on him and after a short diversion to knock the kettle on, came back, sat down, and said "Now, you were telling me about your geography teacher…"

In the end the lady made tea for the rest of the patrol and took it out to them so they could drink it in the outhouse. I stayed by the fire. The patrol commander was ok about what happened when I finally came out, but he didn't let me do any more door knocking if I remember.

As a footnote to this, the farmer's wife asked me if I was going home soon (I was, in about a week) and asked me take something back to give to her daughter. The alarm bells were starting to ring but in fact it was just some letters. I don't know why she didn't just post them, but they were all open so I could see what was inside them, so it's not as if it was a box that was ticking. When I got back to Manchester I fulfilled my promise, saw the young lady at Salford University and handed over the letters. Of course, I couldn't let the side down, so I asked her out on a date and she accepted. And I am NOT going to tell you what happened!

Simon (Trooper) Pickford. 1st Battalion Royal Green Jackets.

"Do you know what a soldier is, young man? He's the chap who makes it possible for civilised folk to despise war."

Allan Massie

Celebrity spotting in Berlin

I joined the army in 1962, enlisting in the Corps of Royal Military Police. My first posting after pass out, as a big bold and brave Lance Corporal was 247(Berlin) Provost company. Duties included town patrols, seeing the squaddies weren't misbehaving, and of course patrolling the borders. These being the Sector Border through the city from SAN Kruger Bridge (start of the French Sector), through to Potsdammer Platz, (beginning of the American Sector). I also patrolled the 'Zonal Border' that ran all around the perimeter of the city. Every 100 metres along the border on the East German side was a manned and heavily armed machine gun tower. These towers were set back from the actual border fence, and between them and the fence was the death strip. This was 200 metres of raked earth liberally seeded with buried or trip activated anti-personnel mines some of which were designed to jump out of the ground and explode at crotch level causing extreme damage to anyone who activated them. Lovely people those East German Border Guards.

The pièce de résistance was having to patrol the Russian war memorial down almost to the Brandenburg Gate, which was about a hundred metres inside East Berlin. We had been informed that the President of the United States, John F Kennedy, was paying a visit to the city, but no one was expecting him to turn up at the Brandenburg Gate.

My oppo and I had just turned into 17th June Strasse leading to the gate, when we saw a group of vehicles. As there was a no parking restriction on this street we went down to see what was happening.

As we got to the observation tower that looked over the wall to the Brandenburg Gate we saw someone up there. I went up to see who it was, and it was JFK himself! He turned to look at me and asked in a very quiet voice if he was in trouble! What could I say?

"No sir" I said, "but it would have been nice to have been informed."

We had a pleasant chat and he asked if could see more of the border so we gave him a guided tour. When it was done, he thanked us profusely and he and the entourage left. After he had gone, I was approached by a member of the American Provost Marshals Office, who invited my pal and me for a drink at their club. We didn't pay for a drink all night and they drove us and our vehicle back to our HQ. A very enjoyable experience if I say so myself.

Not all of our experiences were so positive, in fact, some were extremely unpleasant. One incident ended up with me going on a booze bender and breaking down crying like a baby. It was the time we picked up two teenage boys who had managed to negotiate the death strip and all other obstacles and escape to the West. Because of their age, and their parents complaining to the Western authorities, they had to be returned to the East. We handed them over at an East German checkpoint. The kids were crying. When the bastard border guards got them into East Germany they beat the crap out of the poor buggers. I felt like shooting the fucking shites but my oppo grabbed my machine pistol before I started an international incident. I had a drunk on for a few days.

Chas Bennet RMP

The Brandenburger Tor in 1962 taken by Chas
Bennet. A matter of metres inside East Berlin.

The Brandenburger Tor today

James Bond

I had a crappy old bright yellow Ford Capri that was nicknamed the flying banana. The brakes on it were a bit dodge and getting dodgier, but I was trying to get my money's worth out of them and anyway, that weekend Mark and me were off to Monchengladbach. On the way back I was hammering along at about 70 mph just as the lights changed to red. I hit the brake pedal and was instantly in trouble as the front left wheel locked and the right one didn't. I instantly lost control and we span across the entire road ending up on the wrong side of the road facing the way we had just come. Fortunately for us it was the middle of the night and the roads were completely empty. After the initial shock and the realisation that we had hit nothing, we both cracked up laughing. I said, "Fuck me Mark that was lucky. Good job the old bill ain't about". I spun the car back around and carried on. As I looked into my rear view mirror I could see a newish looking VW Golf flashing his headlights. Game on I thought. Mark agreed.
He said, "Race on mate, this guy wants a go"
I tanked it down the road, the VW still behind me flashing its lights.
As we got onto a long straight I knew the Golf would pass me with ease but it didn't. It just sat behind me flashing its headlights.
The penny dropped.
"Fuck me Mark, I think this guy is a copper."
I pulled over at the next lay-by and sure enough, he pulled in behind me. The uniformed cop got out of his car and started to speak to me in German. The only words I understood were James Bond.
He eventually gave up, got on the radio and called an

English speaking cop to assist.

The second officer arrived and spoke with his colleague. Again the only words I understood were James Bond. The second copper came over with a wry smile on his face.

"So my colleague would like to fine you. He said you drive like James Bond"

So I got the second fine of the day, 20 marks for speeding, to go along with 10 mark jaywalking fine we had both got in Monchengladbach. Considering I motored off and he had to chase me I think 20 marks was a bargain!

Spike Elliott MT/MHE Bracht

A Major problem

Ok, let me set the scene. Towards the end of 2008 I was released from MCTC after getting 120 days and a reduction in rank. Prior to the court martial I had been told I was about to be promoted to sergeant. When I was released, I was posted to 3 Logistics Support Regiments Light Aid Detachment (3LSR LAD). Yep, REME REMF.

I was posted there as a Corporal, but went from Corporal to Lance Corporal to Craftsman in a single day. Ah well. Anyway, the summer of 2009 saw me going to Canada on a Medicine Man exercise, not sure which one but the Royal Welch Fusiliers were the infantry battalion.

We flew out ahead of the main body to prep the vehicles for exercise and someone decided a porn star tache competition was a good idea. One morning parade, third day I think, I was 'promoted' in the field by an RLC driver, Lance Corporal Gurung, or G as we knew the madhead. He had found an old Green Howard's Major rank slide in the

Gag & Puke and had decided that corporal to craftsman was a bit harsh and that I deserved a promotion. Our troop Commander was 2nd Lieutenant called Brown, a legend who gave zero fucks and hated the RLC. He wasn't around for much the exercise. I think he transferred to the AAC to become a chopper pilot shortly afterwards.

So it became a running joke, Major Gaiger. (Major and Gaiger rhymes, so it appealed to the sense of humour.) Going along with the joke, I wore the rank slide on my body armour under my smock and promptly forgot it was there.

About a week into the first exercise we were called to a briefing for the next phase. We were somewhat the worse for wear at the time having been hitting the brown milk quite hard on a daily basis and due to my tipsy state I had not thought to hide my major's rank slide, but this was no issue as the Troopie was on board. But the Troopie wasn't giving the brief. It was the Directing Staff. Oh joy. An RLC WO2 complete with white mine tape on his uniform (marking him out as an umpire), braced up to attention as I entered. Thankfully, I wasn't that bladdered. I simply nodded to him and said "Sergeant major".

I then sat in on the brief, no beret obviously, and having zipped up my old and worn Para smock I tried not to draw too much attention to myself.

After the brief was over the lads ripped me apart with good natured abuse, as you would expect. The senior REME guy under the Troopie was a vehicle electrician turned mechanic, Corporal James Brookes. He couldn't run a bath, never mind a section, nice bloke but he wasn't up to the job. Lance Corporal Gavin Cooke took on the role of running us, albeit unofficially. Now Gav is an AQMS (WO2) based in Canada and the irony of it is not lost on me. Gav and I drove around the prairie in a four ton DAF lorry with a CALM attending breakdowns and the like while trying to appear more sober than we actually were. We attended Battle Group echelon meetings, collected spare parts, fixed vehicles all the time as Major Gaiger and his trusted driver Lance Corporal Cooke. I was fronting out every occasion where people treated me as a Major with more and more ease. Lots of tea was made for me and there was lots of deferential behaviour. All with Cookey looking on laughing. The alcohol helped.

I remember bollocking a young Welsh fusilier on sentry duty for saluting me in the field. We laughed loads about that one, Cookey and I, but I think the high point was when I asked an SSM during a briefing where he expected our supply group to be attacked that afternoon. "I am sure you understand Sergeant Major, I want to ensure that I and my team are in the right place to observe our commander's responses."

Of course, he told me. We never did get bumped, I told the Troopie where it was going to happen, and he turned us off the MSR one turn before its planned location. Ah well.

The exercise finished and then came the awful task of cleaning, inspecting and repairing the vehicles ready to be handed back over to BATUS. I had no job to do, being a vehicle electrician and not allowed to inspect vehicles, so I simply stood out the front of the servicing bay directing the Battle Groups fleet of B vehicles into bays for Cookey, Brookesy and the other lads of my detachment to inspect. They punched their plums in that day, I simply swanned around as a Major directing vehicles into bays receiving endless salutes and giving those awful 'not so much a salute but a wave' type of officer salutes in return.

After the Med Man exercise I decided I had pushed my luck far enough and the rank slide was retired. It disappeared into history and I thought it was gone forever, but incredibly, it reappeared at my dine out when I retired after 22 years in the army as part of an epic presentation. I was also presented with a two page poem that roasted me, naturally, a large photo of me at the servicing bay as the Major with my slide now worn on my smock epaulette, a couple of cap badges, a brass engraved plaque and two Major rank slides including the original Green Howard's one, still folded up to obscure the unit it was from.

It is still spoken about apparently. Two young REME guys on a sailing expedition off the coast of Australia spoke about it to a guy I served with and sailed with, a recovery mechanic called Adam Boffy. They recounted the tale of Major Gaiger one night to the crew of the yacht not aware that Boff knew me, and knew the tale. They were 80% right 6 years after the event. I was a civilian when I found out. Ah... immortality...

John Gaiger

The award to 'Major' Gaiger.

Thirsty work

In the early eighties I found myself stationed in Paderborn, a pleasant city thoughtfully rebuilt after the RAF had flattened 95% of it in World War 2. One day, as a battery, we packed up and headed South-ish to Vogelsang, near Aachen, which has an interesting history if one bothers to research the place; it was the education centre for senior Nazis' children.

By the time I got there the Nazis were gone and it was a training facility for the fine British soldiery that were posted to BAOR. For the most part, and contrary to everyone else's and my own expectations, I had a pretty good time. My late and beloved friend Tez Collins had decided my motivation needed some attention and had taken it upon himself to provide words of encouragement that, to my astonishment, actually worked.

Brushing my beret to the required standard I entered into the spirit of things and adopted an attitude of obedience and compliance, and did my English best until one fateful morning it was decided to send the Battery on a route march.

"Fine." said I, as O Troop bounded on its way into the hills that surrounded Vogelsang. All was going swimmingly well until it became clear our water bottles were going to be hopelessly insufficient. This proved to be the case in short time and became a popular topic of conversation.

After an hour or so someone in the Troop spotted a brook bubbling and chuckling its way through a clearing.

"Aha!" thought some troop members, and we descended upon said brook and drank our fill and filled our bottles. We continued on our march, which we completed about tea time, boarded the Bedford 4 tonners and headed back to Vogelsang.

Now, my story takes a dark turn...

In the Bedford I felt a vague rumbling low down in my innards, and with the natural joie de vivre of youth I attempted to ignore the warning and continue with my evening. This was Saturday. Sunday was spent semi-conscious on my bed.

On Monday I reported sick after the holocaust that had befallen my bowels and my head was another clear indicator that all was not well. Standing in a line with other troop members who had made the same fateful error as me, we exchanged toilet stories, that with each telling became more absurd and life threatening.

My own account of an explosion of liquid mustard coloured faeces that coated my inner legs, lower back and the wretched toilet I was sitting on was met with a mixture of sympathy and scepticism. It was quickly parried by a story of similar challenge.

But time and youth are great healers, and after three days of 'light duties', which is army's way of calling you a skiving twat, myself and the other fools were back on the job.

A short time after this and for reasons known only to whoever decides these things, O Troop were sent on a short weekend exercise to the wooded training ground in Sennelager, which as anyone who was there will know was very close to Paders.

We finished whatever it was we were doing and built a fire. Breaking out those golden handbags of Herforder we settled down for a beer or three. I was mesmerised by the spectacle of my crew commander, Bombardier Tony 'Perv' Reed, working his way through a bottle of either vodka or

101

Bacardi, I forget which, but it was disappearing at an alarming rate.

I decided I needed to urinate and took myself off a short distance and began my errand in the half light of dusk. Enjoying the blessed relief that accompanies a good slash and enjoying the freedom one feels pissing over the undergrowth I glanced up and froze. Before my eyes and no more than ten feet in front of me stood the biggest, blackest and hairiest wild pig I'd ever seen. It stared back. It was a moment of terror and almost hysterical hilarity as I knew that if this thing charged me it would kill me. Following the finest traditions of the Lane family I ran squawking back to the fire to tell my story. The whole troop didn't believe me and Perv laughed like a hyena, telling me I had imagined it.

What I and the rest of the Troop couldn't know at that moment was that for the rest of the night we would all be listening to this pig mooching its way through camp searching for snacks.

Such nostalgia.

This event had a significant effect my bowels too!

Mick Lane J (Sidi Rezegh) Battery

I warned him!

I was posted to 3 Armoured Division Field Ambulance from basic training and was not happy to hear on arrival that we were THE medical NBC training unit for the British Army. This meant all our exercises were done in noddy kit and we would often get sent experimental bits of NBC kit do trials on. Effectively, this meant that no one had the same kit as anyone else and if we paraded in full NBC suits we looked like a bunch of mercenaries from a Star Wars movie. We had respirators with one canister, two canisters, all different suits, boots that looked like wellies, it was all over the place. In 1981 I had a respirator with a single piece of glass rather than the standard issue S6 which had two. The OC also had a funky piece of kit. A microphone that he could attach to his respirator when it wasn't clipped to his belt and a small portable loudspeaker so he could make himself heard when fully kitted up.
On exercise we would set up a double one-way chamber for casualties. A casualty would go into the first one and be decontaminated, then into the second one to be treated. The second chamber had filtered forced air, so the pressure inside was always greater than the pressure outside, relieving the medics inside from the necessity of wearing NBC kit whilst carrying out treatment.
Because you had to be as careful as possible about contamination, you could not enter the clean chamber from the decontamination one, or the decontamination one from the outside and that was that. This guy in the decontamination chamber got bored and kept sticking his head out and pinging stuff off the helmet of my mate who was stood outside on stag, knowing he couldn't do anything like come in and retaliate. My mate told him to

pack it in several times, and fucking meant it. Being in this kit will put you in a pissy mood at the best of times, but he kept doing it. He was dicing with death, my mate was a big guy. I was coming and going doing my normal stuff and every time I passed my mate moaned to me about it, his voice distorted by the respirator, but the rules were very strict. No entry. Finally he said to me, "The next time he puts his head out of there I am going to fucking lump him." A few minutes later a respirator slowly comes out and quick as a snake my mate lets him have it.
The recipient goes flying and the contents of the respirator and noddy suit are laid, spark out on the floor. My mate turned to me and said, "I fucking warned him". True. Then he notices the clip on the belt and the attachment on the ressie.
"Oh... bollocks."
Some helpful soul pointed out that the person couldn't be identified through the glass eyepieces of the ressie as they were smeared with blood. Yes, thanks, but we didn't think this would work as a defence at a Court Martial as the blood probably wasn't there before he got thumped. Still, at least now they had a real casualty to practice on! My mate got 14 days' ROPs for that, which is probably less than you could expect for decking the OC!

Rob P 3ADFA Sennelager

Wife-of and the march out of married quarters without the spouse present

Back in 1967 when I was three, we lived in London where my dad had been attached for some strange reason to a TA unit for 6 months while his regiment were sent over to Germany for a couple of years. My mum was heavily pregnant with my brother and my dad was a young sergeant in the Household Cavalry.

Shortly before the regiment decamped one of the officers got married and my dad and some of his soldiers were to form a guard of honour. I had been in bed for a couple of hours when he turned up, fairly tipsy, with one of his mates in tow.

"You don't mind if Dave crashes here, do you?" he asked my mum who was, unusually for her, still up and sitting in the living room.

"He's welcome to stay, but I'm having a baby."

"Yeah, we know that, but can he sleep on the sofa."

"I'm. Having. A. Baby." My dad nodded. Dave nodded. They both nodded. My mum fixed my dad with an icy stare. "The baby is coming now. Call the midwife."

Back in those days having a phone was a luxury that not many people living in married quarters could afford so my dad ran out of the front door and scooted off down to the end of the street to the phone box. My mum gave Dave a cup of tea and sat him in the armchair, out of the way. She was pretty far along and paced around the small flat practicing the breathing and worrying that she was about to pop out a baby with only a slightly drunk soldier for company. Luckily, I was far away in the land of nod. Meanwhile my dad had arrived at the phone box to find it was out of order, so he had to run to the next one. Finally he managed to alert the midwife who immediately jumped into her trusty mini and by the time he got back home she had arrived, and my mum was in the bedroom with her all ready to produce his son and heir. This she duly did, about fifteen minutes after my dad got back. He ran into the living room to tell Dave the good news, but he'd heard the commotion and was reaching into a paper bag he'd brought with him. The first liquid that passed my brothers lips was champagne purloined from the wedding. A week later the regiment left for Detmold and my mum was left with a 3-year-old and a small baby to pack up their belongings – not too difficult in those days, as each family only got a few MFO boxes, all furniture and fittings were provided back then. She also had to get the flat ready for the handover, the dreaded 'marching out'. Of course, all the wives helped each other and she said that the only thing worrying her was that there was a huge enamel mixing bowl that she didn't use which had been on top of the kitchen cupboards since they had moved in. She had put it in the sink to wash it and the enamel cracked right across from the hot water. The bowl was fine but the enamel looked bad because of the crack, which gave her sleepless nights. On the day of the march out the grumpy old major in charge took look one look at the bowl and tossed it in the bin where it smashed.

"Nobody uses those anyway." he said. And that was that. There was also a set of aluminium pans which she had scrubbed to a shiny finish. He simply bent all the handles back so they couldn't be used with the aside, "Nobody uses those either". Git.

Anon

106

Surprise!

It all started when I was a Private Contractor in Kandahar. Halloween was approaching and with us working closely with the Americans the head shed decided that we would hold a fancy-dress BBQ to celebrate as getting drunk was out of the question.

As you can imagine, getting a costume together in a war zone was a challenge and the brief was 'come as something scary for Halloween'. At this point my plan was hatched. Our translator was tasked with getting me appropriate attire and then we went into action...

Rumours had got out as to what I was planning to do and I got a phone call from my manager. (An old Army buddy who had got me out there.) I was called to his office and when I got there the conversation went as follows;

Me – "Morning Boss. What have I done now?"

Boss – "It's not what you have done, it's *where* you are going to do it and what you are *going* to do."

Me – (Confused) "What I am *going* to do?"

Boss – "Yes."

Me – (More confused) "How do you mean?"

Boss – "Halloween, and no, change your costume."

Me – "Why? It will be funny."

Boss – "No it won't, and you do know where we are don't you?"

Me – "Yes, but come on, it will be a laugh..."

Boss – "I am not authorising it. You can see the Ops Director if you like."

Me – (Disappointed) "Ok."

Now the Ops Director was an ex infantry man of 22 years and a prop forward for many years, he is a big unit by any stretch, a man never lost for words and not easily worried. So off I bimble to see him. I knocked on his door and got called in.

Ops – "Morning! What have you done this time?"

Me – "It's not what I have done but what I want to do."

Ops – "Oh yeah? What's that then?"

Me – "It's the Halloween Party. I want to go as something scary, but the Boss won't let me."

Ops – "Why not? The scarier the better! What do you want to go as?"

Me – "A suicide bomber..."

Cue the pin drop silence and tumble weeds rolling across the office. The Operations Directors jaw dropped in disbelief at what he had just heard. After what seemed like an eternity, he looked me in the eye and said, "What the…. how the fuck…… oh for fuck's sake………you are serious aren't you? Fuck it, ok, but don't leave the compound."

With a local dish dash on and a utility vest rigged with wires and timers I set off to the party. The look on one of our guys face as he came out of the shower to be greeted by me in my costume was priceless and I think he needed another shower afterwards.

The party was a great success and was even better when the American guests arrived. It was funny to work my way behind a new arrival unnoticed and say loudly "Allahu Akbar!" Cue panic ha ha! Luckily for me they were not allowed loaded weapons in our compound because they were a bit trigger happy and their drills were wholly inadequate.

At one point in the evening an American soldier started to have a whinge about "How inappropriate it was" and "didn't I know what was happening outside the wire… blah blah blah." He was overheard by his SSM who gripped him

108

and asked him if he had ever worked with the Brits before. He replied in the negative and the SSM explained to him that we Brits have the sickest sense of humour going, and we do stuff that what have the devil embarrassed, but he would rather fight with us than any other military, as in his words we were 'Sick Badass Motherfuckers'.

An enjoyable evening was had by all. The highlight has to be when they decided to form up for a unit photo to celebrate the night, at which point the best ever photo bomb happened.

Stuart Clarkson

PHOTOBOMB
Level = Suicidal

"Dark sense of humour 'can be dementia warning sign'".

Story by Aidan Radnedge in Metro newspaper.

Happy daze

I had some good times whilst I was soldiering, and the laughs started in basic training at Junior Leaders. We had been given a handbook for patrol signals and were told to read it. We sixteen year olds considered ourselves quite experienced, having been in the army for weeks, but had a quick glance and thought it was all quite basic. Unfortunately I was the one who ended up behind the instructor, a light infantry corporal, when we went out on a night patrol. It was very dark and he signalled me to close in on his position. Because it was so hard to see I interpreted it as a signal to get down, so I went onto one knee. He then gave the signal again. I could tell he was agitated by the movement of his hand so I lay on my belly, a bit confused. He lost his rag and shouted in a whisper "WHO THE FUCKING HELL IS THAT???!!!".

I don't know why I did it, but I said in my best Irish accent "Its Malone Corporal".

A few seconds later my ex-buddy Malone shouted, "It's not me Corporal, I'm over here".

Let's just say that's where that bit of comedy ended.

On one exercise, after I finished basic, I was really knackered so I sneaked off with my sleeping bag and fell asleep in a field. I was woken by the sound of an approaching vehicle, very close. I opened my eyes and the wheel went past my head and then clipped my knees. I woke up in a rush and went looking for somewhere safer to have a kip. Like a minefield. Two years later I was in the QM's reminiscing about funny moments and my boss at the time, Major Ward, said to Corporal Gibson "Remember when we were in a Land Rover crossing a field and we almost killed that fucking idiot in a sleeping bag?"

Gibson roared with laughter and they continued to slag the idiot off. I eventually owned up.

Later, the regiment was sent on tour to the former Yugoslavia. They had banned drinking but I convinced a few of the lads that we could sneak off camp and go to a village a few miles up the road for a sly one. We waited for our chance and made our escape, sticking to the roads and hiding when a vehicle came. The country was still at war but we really, really fancied a beer. We got to the local bar and I went in to order. A few of the local guys in there had weapons, but it felt quite normal to be honest. I ordered four pints in my best Croatian which was four fingers followed by the words "Pivo, Havala". Whilst outside, a group of men approached us and one told us he had been to university in London.

We chatted for a bit, then he said to me "Can you answer a question? Why do you English always want to fight after a drink?"

I took a moment thinking about my reply, fighting back the urge to mention the ethnic cleansing that his people had done recently, guessing that a discussion on these lines would probably lead to a fight and prove him right. I just said that unfortunately some people can't handle their beer. We did this sneaking out for quite a few weeks until we got caught.

The ban on alcohol threatened to put the dampeners on my best mate's 21st birthday. I managed to get loads of spirits and we locked ourselves into out portacabin with the other cap badges on rapid response. I was a decent drinker at the time and claimed I could out drink anyone. The next thing I remember is my WO2 waking me up and screaming at me with the regimental police standing behind him. I opened my eyes. I could see outside through a hole in the wall, the room was trashed and the door had been ripped off. Possibly a bit lacking in credibility, I protested that I was innocent, I just went to bed early. He asked if I thought he was an idiot and pointed down. I looked down. I was wrapped in my sleeping bag, fully dressed and had been sick all over myself. We all spent the next two hours getting beasted round the camp until we threw up. Again.

Craig Kirby

Sometimes this job is murder

While the Cold War was going on in Europe, I was a 'Chairborne warrior' involved in a very hot war in Aden whilst working with the South Arabian Army. I was living in Maalla with my family, on the fifth floor of a block of flats. Maalla was largely made up of blocks of flats housing a large number of British families and it was known as Murder Mile, as murders were an almost daily occurrence. To take the weight off the security forces we were all, regardless of rank, required to do a two hour patrol around our patch every day. Lady luck smiled on me and there were only a couple of incidents on my patch in my whole time there. One tragic incident being when a young Lance Corporal was killed across the road by the oft favoured hand grenade.

One afternoon I did my stag and went home at about 1800 hours. About thirty minutes after I got home a grenade exploded right below my flat, so I rushed to the window to see if I could spot the thrower. People on their balconies were shouting that he had run into the narrow alley below us. I had my rifle in my hand and remembering my bathroom window was open this young, fit, wannabe hero raced through the flat to leap out of it onto the balcony outside. I entered the room at speed and leapt for the closed toilet to use it as a springboard to fly outside Superman like, which would, no doubt, draw gasps of admiration from my deeply impressed neighbours.

Alas, my foot went through the seat and got stuck in the U bend. The butt of my rifle was under my armpit, the dangerous bit pointed aimlessly up to the sky and I was clinging to the window ledge by my fingertips. Viewed from the outside I probably looked like Chad, definitely not Superman.

I had a clear view of the target but pull as I did in those few seconds, I could not extract my wet desert boot and watched as he disappeared into the Trade Union building. An interesting epilogue to the story, and just to prove that the British always play by the rules, the next morning I was telling the story to some mates and laughing about how stupid I must have looked. The acting RSM, who was a cold fish, was there and he said, "If you had killed him, I would have charged you with murder. He was running away with his back to you and you had no proof that he was the person who had thrown the grenade." Cheers sir.

Unbelievably, although there were no more families arriving in the Colony, they still insisted on a 100% check of the contents of the flat. Some months later I was given a bill of £2.10s.0d (£2.50) for damaging the seat. This irritated me so I submitted an appeal to HQ Mideast explaining the situation. They responded saying this monstrous sum had been written off but I was "Not to use army toilet seats as an 'Aiming post' in future."

Bill Coulthard

The Dance of the Flaming Arseholes #2

"Fancy some Adventure training in the Rockies?" my
Troop sergeant asked.

"Don't mind if I do." I replied, not knowing that a couple of
days later my arse cheeks would still feel like they were on
fire.

The Adventure Training was the usual fare of mountain
biking, kayaking and hill walking (normally taken by an
uptight Senior NCO who thought he was still on exercise
and wanted to tab to the top of the hill and the peaks
beyond in double quick time).

Alas we never got as far as the hill walking.

There I was on day one shitting myself that the noise
outside my tent was a grizzly bear ready to use me as its
plaything, knowing full well that the duty bod whose job it
was to make sure that the bears did not enter the camp
was probably asleep. The tents were our accommodation
for the rest of the week as there were only two log cabins,
one for officers and Senior NCO's with as many minions as
possible crammed into the small log cabin that was left.

As the Paras were part of our Battle Group several of them
were in our Adventure Training party. I have got nothing
against our airborne comrades, but all involvement I had
previously had with them had not made me relish their
company. The two times I was with them involved people
shitting in mess tins and challenging each other to see
who could eat the most whilst smearing it over their faces,
and when I was in Cyprus, it was who has got the hardest
forehead by stopping the mahoosive fan in the room with
their head while balancing on a poly prop chair on a
wonky table. Needless to say, the Paras won both
competitions, as the slashed foreheads on first parade

clearly demonstrated. (If memory serves me well, a Para called 'Ox' with a fan speed of 11 was the winner.) Anyway, I digress. Our second day was pretty chilled signing for all the kit we would need for the remainder of the week (alas we never got to use any of it). Then it was down to the local town for a few refreshments. Bearing in mind we had spent the last two months sweating our arses off on the prairie, having a couple or twenty beers was ok... wasn't it?

As with most army organised trips they wisely put the squaddies in the middle of nowhere so it is either on your plates of meat or a Joe Baxi back to camp. Most of us that night got a taxi back. I say most of us, a couple of paras decided it would be cheaper and more fun (they were wrong on both counts) to steal a couple of bikes, that wouldn't have looked out of place on the Antique Roadshow, and cycle back.

The next morning, we were rudely awoken by every cop car, police officer and police dog that the state could muster. I was half expecting a troop of mounted police to come charging around the corner. Putting their maroon T-shirts on back to front was never going to fool the police (the paras tried it though, I shit you not!). After that incident we were all gated.

By the middle of the week, after several days of log-chopping, we were all getting pretty pissed off. Every night the Officers and senior NCO's would go out on the piss and come back in the early hours laughing and joking, but we were to have the last laugh.

One night, just like every other night, we watched resentfully as the officers and SNCO's left, but this time we had a glint in our eyes as it had started to snow. The weather in the Rocky Mountains is always unpredictable and when it snows in Canada it doesn't fuck about. It quickly got really bad and was starting to settle nicely. As the snow continued to build up we went to the bar and got pissed. With boredom setting in and the drinks flowing, the paras challenged us tankies to a game of 'The Dance of the Flaming Arseholes'. I had never heard this game. How hard could it possibly be? I rashly volunteered before the rules could be explained, much to the amazement and amusement of my best mate who knew more about the game than I did, because for once he was speechless. It wasn't until I was handed a long piece of bog roll with the instruction to insert one end up my arsehole that I began to have second thoughts. My confidence wasn't helped when I was introduced to my opponent, Donkey. The Paras in the room went silent and then you could hear a small murmur start

"DON...KEY...DON...KEY...DON...KEY" which got louder and louder until it ended up a full on roar of clapping and cheering.

"DONKEY... DONKEY... DONKEY..."

My armoured brethren could barely muster a whimper in support of me, probably due to the fact that they were laughing so much. The only good news was that if my arse caught fire, I had a fellow tankie standing by as fireman with a pint of lager to extinguish the flames.

So it began. Tweeds around ankles, toilet paper inserted and lit. My strategy was that to have any chance of winning I needed to keep as still as possible to prevent he flames from moving too quickly up towards my bike rack. Thinking that Donkey had probably played this game before, I looked across to see my opponent's tactics. He was leaping around the room and roaring, obviously much encouraged by his maroon mates. It was during this energetic display that I noticed the multiple burn marks on his arse cheeks. Not only had he played this game before, he appeared to have played this game a *lot* before. He appeared to be revelling in the pain as he jumped up and down doing a tribal dance shouting "PARAS....PARAS". By this stage his arse was well and truly on fire. It suddenly dawned on me that I was never going to win this competition as I am a normal person whose arse is about to go up in flames.

Mentally conceding defeat, I tried to grab the bog roll and pull it out but it burned my hand, so I screamed at my fireman to put me out. The fact that I had lost the competition and that Donkey had won didn't seem to have much effect on him. He carried on dancing and yelling and appeared to be actually enjoying himself!

Well, I lost, but on a positive note at least I didn't have to do any mountain biking.

Most people then made moves to go to bed forgetting the return of the pissed up officers and Senior NCO's. We didn't.

The officers all returned later in the night when most of us, but not all, were fast asleep. I heard them talking and laughing loudly as they went towards their log cabin uncaring about the fact they might disturb our beauty sleep, and let's face it, Donkey needed all the beauty sleep he could get. Their laughter soon stopped, right around the time they realised that we had built a huge snow wall covering all doors and windows into their log cabin. Snow walls which, if you have seen Game of Thrones, were like the ice wall on the northern border of the Kingdom in the North.

Being wide awake now, but like several co-conspirators ready to feign sleep, I heard them talking in tones I would describe as utter dismay. They went around in verbal circles for a bit until a future Field Marshall said, "Well, we will just have to dig our way in".

Good luck with that, I thought, thinking of the treeline where all the spades in the camp had been hidden away. Warm and comfortable, I drifted slowly off to sleep with a smile on my face but a very sore arse.

Trooper Donaldson 1RTR

"We were probably the fittest alcoholics in the world."

Anonymous British soldier

Ok to go live

When I was BSM of 211 Battery the whole of 104 Regiment RA went to practise live firing Javelin, a short range, hand held, anti-aircraft missile at Manorbier Missile range on the Pembrokeshire coast.

During the live missile firing I was the Visual Flight Safety Officer (VFSO) which sounds very important and complicated. Important yes, complicated no. You sit in the range control tower looking through a small black square frame which represents the arcs the missile has to stay in. If it wanders out of arc you flick a switch and the missile self-destructs, simple.

On this occasion there was the Director of Practice, Major 'H' and me in one room but the control room next door was much busier. In there was the radar operator, the range WO2 'TP', the target drone operators and the reps from Shorts, the company that make the javelin missiles.

On any live firing exercise there are always VIPs who turn up to enliven what would otherwise be a dull day in an office so we also had the Master Gunner from the school of Artillery at Larkhill WO1 'PM' who had dropped in to dodge his routine paperwork.

At this point I must stress that as far as the missile is concerned, the VFSO (me) is only responsible for cutting down the missile if it wanders out of the arcs, nothing else. The only other duty I had was to relay by radio the information and instructions from the Director of Practice (DOP) and Sergeant Major Instructor Gunnery (SMIG) which is broadcast over an internal PA system so everyone in the control complex can hear what is going on.

This day everything is going great. There were six firers, six hits and then a local Greenpeace councillor decides to park his boat in the middle of our arcs for a spot of fishing.

That's it. RANGE CLOSED.

To remind the people in the control room of the range status there is a slider box in the window that has two colours. RED (Range Closed) on the left, and Green (Range open) on the right. The DOP slides it to Red. Before an operator gets to fire a live missile costing tens of thousands of pounds he/she has to complete 1000 practice shots on simulator achieving a miss distance of three metres or less, then on the day do a dry run which must be perfect.

This day was a first for the regiment as there was a female firer, Bombardier 'O'. We gave Bombardier 'O' a few dry runs and after about an hour she has had five attempts and is getting it right.

The SMIG announces, "OK to go live".

In the excitement everybody in the control room has forgotten that the range is closed. I relay the message as I should and the FPO announces, "Loading live missile, number 1234."

The DOP checked it is the correct missile allocated to the correct firer and announced, "Run starts."

The operator acquired the target in the monocular sight and shouts, "HOSTILE!"

The FPO shouts, "ENGAGE!"

The missile fires.

A few seconds later the Range WO2 burst in, pointed at the slider in the window and shouted, "THE FUCKING RANGE IS CLOSED!!"

The DOP looked at me, I looked at him, and we both burst out laughing. This cannot be happening, but happening it is. At this point the Master Gunner and the SMIG both sneaked out of the back door and come back in 30 seconds later demanding to know what had happened. I imagine they started writing their statements whilst they were out there; "Sir, at the time of the incident I was on the rear fire escape having a fag when I heard a missile going down the range. On entering the control room I saw the Range WO2 explaining to the DOP that the range was closed."

The DOP, the Master Gunner, the SMIG and the SPSI were all looking extremely worried. In jest I said to them "You can blame me. I'm TA and have no career or pension to lose." It didn't cheer them up.

Later that day I was approached by a certain SMIG who explained that a Board of Enquiry was going to be convened, and that its purpose was not to apportion blame but to make sure it never happened again. He shifted his feet uncomfortably and said it would be better if I didn't mention in my statement that the order to go live was actually given by the DOP and the SMIG.

We heard afterwards that the missile nearly blew the councillor out of his boat. Any javelin cloud puncher will tell you that the first stage motor blows the missile out to a distance of about 300 metres whereupon the warhead is armed, then the missile drops considerably before the second stage motor propels it to mach 2. This is where the missile was at (and quite close to the councillor) when it was aborted. Serve him right for spoiling our day.

There are a few people involved in this story that can thank their lucky stars that TA Tel kept his word. When asked by the Lieutenant Colonel on the Board of Enquiry a

few months later "Did the DOP or SMIG say at any time while the range was closed 'Ok to go live?'".
"No sir." I lied.
And that was it. Endex. No more said. March out Sergeant Major.

TA Tel. WO2 in a Welsh TA Air Defence Battery

I like to ride my bicycle...

In the late 1980s I was stationed with one 1 RHA in Hohne when we had a new assistant adjutant posted into the Regiment. She was absolutely gorgeous and everyone looked forward to giving her a good saluting whenever they could, and after saluting, in true squaddie fashion, the saluter would turn and enjoy watching her shimmying off into the distance. She lived in the officers' mess and every day she would ride her bicycle from there to RHQ and leave the bike outside one of the rear doors until she finished work at the end of the day. At least she did, until a certain incident happened.
Some of the lads used to kid each other about sniffing the bike seat after she left it, and a few did, much to the amusement of their mates.
One day she rode her bicycle to work and left it leaning up against the wall outside RHQ as normal, but as soon as she got off and disappeared inside, a pervy gunner ran across to the bike and gave the saddle a long and appreciative sniff. Unfortunately for him, and for reasons unknown, the owner had come back out of RHQ almost as soon as she had gone in and caught him doing it.

125

She absolutely freaked out and was yelling at the stunned gunner who had nothing much to defend himself with. Things got worse for him after that when the RSM heard the commotion and came out of his office to see what was going on. He was told by a very upset assistant adjutant what had happened and the RSM had the guy quick marched to the Guard Room by the RP's. He was banged up for a while, but I don't remember how long. I know this because a mate of mine was one of the RP staff. I can't remember if it ended there, but if it didn't, I would love to know what they charged him with.

Bombardier anonymous. 1 RHA.

A Blast from the Past

Whilst I honestly make the claim that my sense of humour is not normally of a lavatorial nature I submit the following true anecdote for your perusal, and may it give you all a laugh.
Whilst serving in Cyprus in the late 50's our accommodation was in tents so there was not much privacy afforded us and individual habits were very much noticeable and to the fore. One squaddie sharing our four man home had a very amusing habit, not uncommon in the British Army. He would lie on his bed with a towel draped over him for modesty then suddenly raising his thighs, he would emit a tremendous fart! Not content with just carrying out this function he would have ready in his hand a lighter which at the critical moment he would use to ignite the obnoxious fumes. He was very proud of this artistic

display and would sometimes hone his skills by attempting to play a tune with his farts and have us guess what the melody was. Such musical talent!

One day he ignited a particularly impressive anal blast and produced the biggest blue flame and explosive sound to date. We were impressed and about to congratulate him on reaching new heights with his performance when he screamed in agony. He was howling in pain crying, "OH ME BOLLOCKS!!" Not only that, he had burnt off some of his pubic hairs and set fire to his bedding.

Falling about in hysterics we watered him down and got him off to the Medical Inspection (M.I.) room. Then, like the good mates we were, legged it, leaving him to explain the incident. My unit did not have its own M.I. room so we had to use 2 Para's, who were stationed nearby. The para orderly was an eighteen stone gorilla, who I knew from previous experience as he treated me for a septic finger. When he was giving me an antibiotic injection he didn't insert the syringe in the normal way, but used it like a dart leaving me with bruises the size of saucers on my bum. It could have been worse I suppose, he could have scored a bullseye. The lad with the burnt balls was a scouse with a brilliant sense of humour and he returned to us shortly after we had dropped him off with a chastened expression and a funny walk. As far as I know he never repeated that particular form of entertainment again and took up crocheting. That last bit's not true of course.

Corporal Ian (Flash) Gordon Royal Sigs.

The Shah and a taxi

The 8th May 1959 was going to be a very interesting day for me and many others in London. Working in a small comcentre in London one of our tasks was to man various signals duties with the parades and ceremonies occurring in the city.

This occasion was the State Visit to the UK of The Shah of Iran and his beautiful wife Empress Saroya who were to be greeted by H.M. Queen Elizabeth and the Duke of Edinburgh at Victoria railway station. The plan was to have the 21 Gun Royal Salute once they had stepped down from the Royal Train onto the platform. The Salute would be performed by The Kings Troop RHA who were positioned in Green Park and had to be perfectly timed with the arrival of the Royal party.

The plan was that a Royal Signals wireless operator would be positioned in the roof above the arrival platform of the Royal train and would report verbally when the Shah and his wife had stepped onto the platform and were about to meet Queen Elizabeth's party. The Shah was given a code name and the operator would say, "Red seven arrived NOW over", for example. This message would pass via my radio relay wireless directly to the Gunners of Kings Troop RHA positioned in nearby Green Park. They would then immediately proceed with the 21 Gun Salute. My radio was back-up for the relay and designated Control for this task.

We had tested the radio comms many times in previous weeks to ensure that the method was reliable. As Horseguards was the HQ of London District and the home of the General Officer Commanding it was thus designated as the responsible party for this operation. Earlier I had taken the radio to a second floor room in the Horseguards building overlooking Whitehall and ran the routine tests. The set was quite easy to use with pre-set frequencies controlled by a switch so it was easy to change frequency without having to re-tune. As it turned out this could almost be said to 'save the day'!

Come the morning of Great Day I arrived at my position in my well-ironed uniform to find it crowded with very senior officers, red tabs abounded! All were fascinated by my 'wireless set' and I impressed them with frequent and carefully rehearsed radio checks. I switched frequencies and radio checked with great abandon and panache.... ho ho...! At that time I was not a trained radio operator, but having said that a well-trained chimpanzee could have done the switching part just as skilfully. Nevertheless the 'brass' seemed to be impressed as I heard murmurs of approval; their butlers presumably switched their wirelesses on and off for them!

The situation grew tense as the station operator quietly reported the train coming to a standstill. I relayed this information verbally to the onlooking top brass as only the most senior officer and I had headsets and the radio did not have a speaker system. The station operator announced, "Carriage door open...(pause)...Red Seven approaching doorway...", and then it happened... a loud crackling cockney voice burst onto the frequency, "Hey guvnor, I've got one 'ere for Feltham...can I..."

I almost screamed into the handset, "All stations, switch to three, repeat three, acknowledge."

Immediately, as rehearsed, Alpha Two and Alpha Three answered, "Roger, over", and changed frequencies. I immediately made a radio check and received acknowledgements. A minute or so later the

Shah and his wife were standing on the platform and the roar of the RHA guns echoed round the City. Wearing headsets, only myself and the senior officer heard this radio interference although my 'audience' would have seen and heard my actions as they were standing nearby. Oddly, we had never experienced such radio interference during our test runs!

I probably had one of the finest views in London of the Royal Party as their beautiful horse-drawn open Landau carriage passed below my second floor
window accompanied by the glittering troop of
The Sovereign's Escort of Household Cavalry. I could literally look down into the laps of the Royal party. Even the TV cameras could not do that! For one time only in my life I had one of the best seats in the house!

To this day I remain unconvinced that our radio net was the only one covering the event. I suspect we were a back-up to a parallel and more sophisticated system unknown to us. However, we did not know that at the time and we did our job professionally and to the best of our ability.

I got a few, "Well done old chap!" from the onlookers as they scrambled off to meet the Shah.... or more likely to the mess for very large G and Ts! I shut the net down, stowed the radio, changed to civvies and headed home to Isleworth....I didn't think the Shah had planned to have a chat with me anyway!

John R. Royal Signals.

Happy birthday to me!

My 21st birthday. We started drinking in the MT driver's rest room at 13:30 on the Friday afternoon, a very heavy session. By the time we got to the NAAFI bar I was already pretty pissed. In the NAAFI bar all the top shelf spirits were numbered one to nine and the tradition was that you drink your regimental number. I suppose the trick is to have a lot of zeroes. Now the thing is, in NAAFI bars in Germany all the shots were doubles. Your army number is 8 digits (for anyone who doesn't know) so 16 shorts works out at almost a pint. There I am, already pissed, drinking my number down in one which I managed to do without puking. (Which was a bonus!) About 6pm my boss walks in the bar.

"Spike, regimental number time. Come on."

"I've already done it boss." said I.

"Not in front of me."

So I drank my second regimental number of the afternoon session, again down in one without puking. (I'm pretty proud of that achievement, as it wasn't unknown for guys to immediately throw up what they had just drunk.) After that I remember nothing, but the next day everyone was more than happy to fill in the missing bits of what happened.

I staggered off to my bed, stripped naked and climbed in. (I always sleep that way.) Absolutely out of it, I was completely unaware that the lads came over to the block, picked me up in my bed, and carried me back to the NAAFI bar bed and all, dropping me a number of times along the way. Me, dead to the world, I didn't even notice.

I woke up around nine–ish, sat up in bed and looked around the NAAFI bar with a 'this isn't my room look on my face'. Then I noticed the bar and, so I am told, I walked straight up to it and ordered a pint. Apparently I got the hump that the whole bar was laughing at me, but looking back its understandable I suppose. I was stood bollock naked at the bar, ordering a drink and having no way of paying for it. Really, having no cash on me was the least of my problems. Thankfully a few of my friends bought me drinks. (*Friends – really? Jonno DP*) Eventually I said I was going for a sleep and wandered, still nekkid as a jaybird, back to the block. When I got there (yes, you have been paying attention haven't you?) I was reminded by its absence that my bed and quilt were still in the bar. Off I went back to the NAAFI to fetch it, and the lads carried it back for me whereupon I fell into deep intoxicated sleep. How I didn't die of alcohol poisoning/exposure/embarrassment I do not know.

I think it's fair to say BAOR soldiers in my time were high functioning alcoholics. It was considered a sin to miss shutter parade. In our case the shutters going up not down.

Spike Elliott MT/MHE Bracht 1987-1990

Spikes is currently writing a book about his life and it will be published under the title 'Mike Echo 4 Alpha'.

"Pain is the feeling of weakness leaving the body. Unless you've served. Then it's probably arthritis."

Anon

A WRAC in BAOR. Wintex 2

The army wasn't really set up for great waves of women arriving. (Well... there weren't that many but that's what it felt like to the regiments in BAOR who were suddenly getting a lot more of them.) 16 Signal Regiment, headquartered in Krefeld, had to take some DTGs and switchboard ops, and while they could put five of them in the Comcen, it left a few to be distributed into the two troops (F and J troops) in 3 squadron.

For those of us who were sent there it meant doing all the exciting soldiery things the men did, for less money of course. Things like sweeping leaves, painting wagons, painting the troop, sweeping leaves... and the occasional exercise. Whenever we were on exercise it was cold. Cold and wet or very cold and dry, often with snow on the ground. It seemed to go cold, colder, Wintex. One Wintex I was out with my usual small detachment of Land Rover, radio relay wagon and generator, and our Comcen box body wagon which was a 3 ton Bedford. Wintex was one of those exercises that seemed interminable at the time but in reality was probably only seven or eight days. This meant that there was always a weekend where we had to get off the roads and join a larger unit. (Trucks are not allowed on German highways after 2200 hours on a Friday and before 00:01 on Monday). On this occasion we were directed to join several other detachments in a German army barracks at Coesfeld.

Friday traffic being what it is we arrived at the camp gates very late in the evening. It was my turn to sit in the co-driver's seat in the Comcen truck and, as I was the best German speaker present, I jumped out with my SMG, to speak to the young guard when we pulled up at the gate. Back then in the mid-80s the Germans still had conscripts in their army. You could identify them immediately as they all had horribly shaven heads and were usually spotty young youths in between school and university or an apprenticeship. As I approached the guard he stopped dead in his tracks and looked at me with a wide-eyed stare. His mouth opened and closed like a guppy, obviously unable to make a sound.

I went with a friendly, "Guten Abend, sau kalt, oder?" But he just turned on his heel and fetched his corporal who took a few seconds to gather his wits. He consulted a list and told us to follow the private, who would walk us to the wagon park. Having been sitting in a cab for a few hours I welcomed the chance to stretch my legs, as well as practise my German, and walked alongside the young soldier, like those men who used to have to walk in front of cars holding a red flag in olden times. It took us more than quarter of an hour to cross the enormous camp and in that time he didn't get up the courage to say one word to me. I later discovered that the WRAC berets, which were dark green, made us look like fierce marines who ate little conscripts for breakfast. This may have explained his reticence. That and the fact that at that time women weren't allowed in the Bundeswehr so most conscripts never saw a woman in uniform.

I waited with the silent private until the German MT sergeant had supervised the parking of our wagons. Finally, when everyone had finished sorting the vehicles and had gathered outside his office he came over with a list and looked at us. I was with the other WRAC (let's call her "A") who was fiddling with her beret. She had a mass of bright blonde curls and was shoving it back under her headgear. The sergeant looked down at his list, counted us again, ran his finger down his list and sucked his teeth as if disappointed. Finally he signed, put the list in his pocket and said, "Follow me." So we did.

He took us to the gym which at that time of night was pretty much in darkness except for a few lights in the foyer. In the dim glow from the soda lights that came through the high-up windows we could see rows and rows of sleeping bags, mostly with snoring British soldiers in them, but a few people were sitting up organising their packs or taking off their boots. The sergeant pointed to the far corner where, luckily for us, there was enough room for our detachment. I took off my boots and shoved them next to my pack, rolled my jumper and combat jacket up as a pillow and crawled gratefully into my sleeping bag. "A" was fidgeting in her sleeping bag beside me but stopped when she had sorted out whatever the issue was. Pretty soon the only sound in the hall was the gentle breathing of hundreds of sleeping soldiers with the occasional snore.

I woke up in the morning when a football landed on me – so I untangled myself from my sleeping bag and chucked it back. The gym was full of people going about their morning business; putting on their boots, rolling up their sleeping bags, coming back from the shower – showers! There were showers! There was even a game of football going on at the other end of the gym. I really, really wanted a shower but I could see that there were no other women, and given the reaction of the sergeant the previous evening it seemed highly unlikely that any of the ablutions had been designated for the use of women only.

I'd need a wingman (wingwoman?), so I nudged "A" and told her to get a move on while there was still the chance of hot water. "A" sat up and stretched. Her sleeping bag was unzipped and fell to her waist.

It was at this point that I realised all the fidgeting in her sleeping bag the previous evening was her removing all her clothes except her bra. The gym grew increasingly quiet as the guys realised that there was a blonde bombshell in the corner wearing underwear and possibly little else. "A" quickly ducked into her sleeping bag and put the rest of her clothes on. We managed, with the help of our own detachment, to get showered and dressed without any problems other than some rather off-colour comments which were pretty much par for the course for a WRAC on exercise anyway.

We'd got our kit packed up ready to bug out (you never knew if there were going to be any weekend 'fun' extra military training on these things) when we noticed a few salutes and "Morning sirs," going on. Our OC came over and explained that he'd been having breakfast in the mess when an agitated German lieutenant had squeaked that there were "Lady soldiers in with all the men," and he'd immediately realised that it was us.

"Sorry, I'm used to thinking of you all as my troops, I forget that some of you are different," he explained before telling "A" and me to follow him to our new accommodation for the rest of the weekend. We'd been allocated a six-man room in the sergeants' mess complete with ensuite ablutions. Bliss.

In the time it took us to dump our packs and use the facilities some comedians had visited and our door and plastered it with pictures from porn magazines. We used our chinagraph pencils to give them all bikinis. And moustaches.

Anon

Things you thought you knew #3

Britain's first nuclear strike force was the V bombers.

In the 1950s the RAF brought into service three large aeroplanes that had the task of dropping nuclear bombs on targets in the event of a third world war. The three bombers were the Vickers Valiant, which entered service in February 1955, the Avro Vulcan, which entered service in May 1956, and the Handley Page Victor, which entered service in November 1957 and they were collectively known as the V Force.

The V force reached its peak in June 1964, when 50 Valiants, 70 Vulcans and 39 Victors were in service. But incredibly they were not actually the first British nuclear strike force...

On the 6th of August 1945 an American B29 Superfortress dropped an atomic bomb on Hiroshima, but it was nearly a British aircraft that did it. If politics hadn't overruled military practicality it would have been a British plane from the 'Black Lancaster' squadron, a unit still shrouded in secrecy almost eighty years after the attack. Why, you may ask, would the British government care about concealing something that happened so long ago? It's a good question. At the beginning of each year the government publishes papers which have been kept secret for the past 30 years, the so called '30 year rule'. But some of the most sensitive documents will remain secret for several more decades. If a record is judged too sensitive by a government department then it can apply to 'extend closure' until 40, 75 or even 100 years have passed. Some may never be revealed. For example, a box of papers relating to the abdication crisis in 1936 was recently held back until 2037, much to the annoyance of historians. There are civil servants who have privately admitted that if they have no legal avenue to block the release of still sensitive documents the shredder has the last word.

So why did the Americans have difficulty? The first bomb was codenamed Little Boy and was planned to be dropped on an undamaged Hiroshima. (The Americans had left it undamaged so they could see how effective their bomb was.) It weighed just under four and a half tons and was ten feet long. The second bomb, earmarked for Nagasaki, was codenamed Fat Man and was even heavier, weighing just over four and a half tons and was six inches longer. During the development of the bombs it was realised that the only bombers in service, the B17 and the B24 couldn't carry this much weight. Fortunately, the B29 Superfortress was in production and could carry the weight, but there was a problem. The B29 had two bomb bays that were separated by the wing spar which took the stress from the wings and obviously could not be removed. But each bomb bay was not large enough on its own to carry the bomb. With the spar in place you couldn't carry the bomb, but if you removed the spar the plane would fold up in flight.

Once informed of the problem Boeing immediately began work to rectify the problem but warned it wouldn't be quick and may, indeed, be impossible. The work on the atomic bomb was progressing quickly and it looked quite likely that there may be a situation where there was a viable nuclear bomb, but no way to deliver it.

Except there was a tried and tested aircraft that could, the British Lancaster.

The Lancaster carried the largest bomb load of any aircraft during the war in its single, long, deep bomb bay. Some of the bombs it delivered were the five and a half ton Tallboy, and the amazing *ten ton* Grandslam, both designed by Barnes Wallis, the inventor of the famous bouncing bomb. Taking the weight was no problem, the only mod that had to be done was removing the bomb bay doors.

The British air ministry realised that it may become necessary for Britain to deliver the attack on Japan if the Americans were unable to deliver modified B29's in time, so a super-secret RAF bomber squadron was formed. RAF Enstone, tucked away in rural Oxfordshire, was selected as the base for this squadron and the unit was called The Black Lancasters. Six aircraft that had the bomb bay doors removed and with no unit markings or insignia of any kind were sent there to train in 1943. The base was already the home of 21 Operational Training Unit flying Wellington bombers, but the two units were kept completely separate and unless flying the Lancasters were kept in their hangars, which were heavily guarded by the RAF police. No known records exist for the eighteen months the Lancasters were at RAF Enston. Officially, they were not there and even in off duty hours were kept separate from other RAF personnel on the base.

By mid-October 1944 the first three modified American B29 bombers were delivered and crews immediately began training to deliver the atomic bombs. The modified bombers were codenamed 'Silverplate' and the trials were a failure. The weight of the dummy bombs bent the airframes causing the bombs to be released before the bomb bay doors were opened.

The raid, if it was going to happen, was not going to be easy for the Lancasters though and the biggest problem would be lack of range. The Lancaster's round trip range of only 2,530 miles was not enough, so years ahead of its time, an air to air refuelling system was designed by the RAF, and successful tests were carried out in November 1944. The government ordered 500 Lancasters to be quickly converted to tankers.

Given the situation the time had come for final plans to be made, but here the politics trumped the practicalities. The British formally approached the Americans and told them that they a trained unit with the right capabilities and equipment ready to go. The Americans, in the shape of Major General Leslie Groves, the American Commander of the Manhattan project, was furious at the thought that a British aircraft may even be considered for the mission to deliver an American atomic bomb.

It's an interesting historical side note that the Manhattan Project, the undertaking to create an atomic bomb, wasn't just American. Britain had been working on a similar project early in WW2 and the Americans had suggested they pool staff and resources and share the results. After full cooperation from the British scientists working in America for years to develop these weapons the Americans refused to share it once it was successful. After World War two ended the British atomic scientists had to return home and start again from scratch, only developing a British nuclear bomb in the early fifties. Privately, Groves did admit to General Hap Arnold, Commander US air forces in the Far East, that if it wasn't possible to modify the Silverplates successfully, they would have no choice but to use the British aircraft. Arnold furiously replied to Groves that it would be an American plane to deliver an American bomb, which begs the question, what would the yanks have done? Would the Americans have redesigned the B29 completely, which would have taken about a year? Unlikely. Would they have asked to borrow some Lancasters so Americans could do the raid? Churchill would have likely refused. Would Truman have overruled Arnold and asked Britain to do it? Probably.

In the end the Silverplates were hurriedly (and not altogether safely) modified and the history came out the way we are familiar with. The Enola Gay dropped Little Boy on Hiroshima on the 6th of August 1945 and Bockscar dropped Fat Man on Nagasaki on the 9th of August. Eighteen months after its formation the Black Lancaster squadron was quietly disbanded.

Researched and written by Jonno DP

Should I stay or should I go?

Over New Year 1964 I managed to get leave so off I went to Scotland (I am a Jock), had an absolutely brilliant time, met a girl and decided not to go back. At first I didn't really care, I was enjoying myself so much, but as time progressed I started to worry more and more. The Army doesn't shrug its shoulders about soldiers going AWOL, they never stop looking for you, and WHEN they find you, they will make an example of you to dissuade others from doing the same. Several days in I had a brilliant idea! What if I get a sick chit from my family doctor to say I am too ill to travel? So off I went to see my local GP with a 'sore back'. I went in and explained my situation, and that I was now officially AWOL he was very understanding and informed me he was ex Royal Navy, and that he completely understood. We chatted in a friendly way for a bit and then he gave me a 'we both know the score' look and asked if it actually hurt.

"Not really," I admitted.

The doctor absolutely exploded, called me a malingerer and told me to get out of his office.

So there I was.

AWOL.

No sick chit.

In the shit.

Again.

Only one thing I can do. Go back to Detmold and take it on the chin.

It was a long journey and I ended up on a wooden seated milk train pulling into Detmold Bahnhof at 5.30am. A quick walk up the hill to Hobart barracks, and with the calmness of a condemned man who has accepted his fate, I had a wash, changed into my uniform and went up to the workshops for morning roll call. My name was called, I answered, and that was it.

Nothing happened...

Nobody yelled at me, no one looked at me funny, no "By the left, to jail, quick maaaarch! Leftrightleftrightleftright...

A week AWOL and nobody had even noticed. Strange as it may sound, after the initial feelings of relief and joy had

143

passed I had mixed feelings about being so insignificant that no one had noticed that I got extra leave!

Derek Grater REME
Keep your beak(er) out

Whilst a senior instructor attached to 159 Regiment RLC in 2008 I was training TA units for operations and I reported to RSM Mathew W*** who was a regular like me.
RSM W*** was one of those persons that if you'd been to Tenerife he'd been to Elevenerife, and was always telling us how great he was. In reality he was one of those guys who had all the gear but little idea, and was irritating to deal with, but obviously we couldn't say or do much about it. Anyway, another instructor nicknamed him Beaker after the character from the Muppet show and the name stuck. Beaker the character would only communicate with the words "Me me me" so it was quite apt. Beaker was never aware of this nickname until the fateful night of the Annual Sergeants Mess Function...
I was the PEC of the mess and Daz, a Sergeant Major, was President of the Mess Committee and we arranged for the function to take place at the Park House Hotel in Shifnel, near Telford. The function was the usual with entertainment, speeches and a money tree. I booked a band but wanted a drag queen to spice up the money tree and give out prizes. Initially Daz was reluctant to go for a drag queen but relented and I booked this chap Tony who sounded great. I met Tony before the function and went through some things. We spoke about how to run the money tree and he agreed to do it during part of his act. He asked who the main personalities were and I told him about the Colonel who, as the highest rank in the room,

144

should be targeted at every opportunity. The colonel was a good guy and would accept any attention received in good humour. I made a point of telling Tony about Beaker, and why he was called Beaker but asked that he be targeted subtly and just feed it in over the night. Tony was eager to get going and said he couldn't wait to meet all the soldier boys.

At the function I was sat with Beaker, Mrs Beaker, the Colonel and his wife, Daz and his wife but I can't remember the stage name Tony used, I really can't. He was a short bald English guy and he got dressed up in a big sparkly dress, huge wig and really high heels. In his drag outfit he was as tall as Big Bird from sesame Street which was funny because he wasn't that big in reality so it was a stunning transformation. I do remember that he was booked through a specialist company called Boogieland near Telford; they are still there.

Tony comes on for the money tree and was hilariously vulgar. He would get bitchy with the ladies as real ladies do, and try and snog the fit soldier boys if they won prizes. After the money tree he started targeting people, chatting up the 'handsome soldiers' and generally keeping everyone on their toes.

He walked over to Beaker, banged both of his hands on his shoulders and said, "Mathew W*** come with me," and got him out of his chair and up on the stage. Tony wasn't subtle and basically humiliated Beaker on stage telling him about his nickname and why we he was called it. When he was finished Beaker scuttled back to his seat, and Tony moved onto someone else.

Whilst Beaker was getting the attention on stage other mess members were giving me their attention and saying I was done for. I started to worry then that I may have gone a bit far. Ah fuck it. What's done is done. What can he actually do to me?

At the interval Beaker had a go at me for being made to look a twat and wanted Tony told that a complaint was going to be made to Boogieland. Beaker also went over to Tony after he left the stage and had a go at him too. I was drunk and with the 'Ah fuck it' feelings that alcohol so usefully encourages I told Beaker to man up and walked away. I went over to check that Tony was ok, he was fine, he just laughed and said, "I can see now why he's called Beaker".

During Tony's next slot he informed the whole function that concerns have been raised about his vulgar language amongst other things, and advised everyone to liaise with me to forward the complaints on to his manager Michelle. He then targeted Beaker again, and again, and again, and also dragged in his wife calling her Mrs Beaker. He started being sexually vulgar and bitchy to her and I thought "I'm really stuffed now," so I just got more drunk to ease the pain that's going to come my way and avoided Beaker for the remainder of the night after Tony finished his stint.

After the weekend it was back to work and Beaker was eager to get hold of me. I was 'too busy' to take his calls but eventually I ran out of excuses and had to speak to him. Beaker initially started by talking about the Afghan package, but in the back of my mind I'm thinking, "Cut to real conversation you want to have mate".

Finally, Beaker said, "The function. How did you think THAT went?" I said to him I thought the drag act was a great idea even if vulgar but acknowledged it may not have been for everyone.

I was then dumbfounded because Beaker said it was great night and I should take credit for it. I couldn't believe I was talking to the same guy. I later found out from the CO's driver that when he took the CO, Beaker and their wives home, the CO would not stop talking and laughing about the drag queen. He had LOVED the night.

So in the end Beaker couldn't really make a thing of it and discipline me. If the CO liked the night he was screwed, so he just slithered away and accepted it. Funnily enough there were no other complaints from anyone else, just Beaker being Beaker.

Michael Kettrick

"*Some people lead 'nothing' lives. The most interesting thing they ever do is die. Thank god for eccentrics.*"

Spike Milligan

The Army needs me!

I joined the army in 1990 as a young spotty faced kid. My last school exam was on the Friday, I had the weekend off, then my dad dropped me off at Manchester train station on the Monday. The train took me south and I got off at Winchester to start basic training at our Junior Leaders depot.

After Juniors I went to my Battalion in Osnabruck and because the staffing and manning levels were all over the place I was sent to the mortar platoon. Usually you had to do at least three years in a rifle platoon before you could get sent to the mortars because it was considered a perk of seniority. Most of the guys were pads in their thirties, so I had to grow up pretty quickly; rather than going on the piss every weekend I was going round their house for barbecues and babysitting. I was a bit nervous about joining the battalion to be honest because I had heard some stories in basic training that suggested there were some nutters there. Someone in the battalion I was getting posted to had wanted to get out of the army but they wouldn't let him. So, he got a bit angry and drove a 432 into the CO's office.

So it's fair to say that I was worried about what I was going to find when I got there, but in fact they were an amazing bunch of lads. Shortly after I arrived we were sent on a Northern Ireland tour, but because I was so young I wasn't allowed to patrol the streets until I had turned 18. When enough time had ticked by (described as Continuation Training by the battalion) I was sent to join the rest of the mortar platoon in a place called Newtown Hamilton.

I was as keen as fuck and totally army barmy which didn't go down well with the sweats in the mortar platoon, so in good army style they set up a windup that was both elaborate and funny and earned me the nickname Trooper.

One day I was walking past the Company office when someone said "I think that there might be something on the noticeboard that could interest you."

The notice said that the Special Air Service and 14 Int Company required someone young to go undercover and pose on a building site as a novice brickie to gather intelligence. Of course, I was sceptical at first being all of 18 but several people encouraged me to do it, saying no one would think an 18 year old would be undercover and that I should go and see the boss. I went to his office and knocked on his door. He called me in and I threw one up. He asked me what I wanted and I told him I'd like to go for this undercover job as it seems like a good opportunity. He considered me for a bit, then said "Yeah ok. I'll put you forward. Leave it with me for a couple of days." A couple of days later he called me back in the office and said "We've been told you are an ideal candidate for this Pickford, we are just waiting for some dates".

Of course, I'm bigging myself up to everybody going, "This is so cool I'm going to be working with the SAS!!" If you have served in the military you are probably shaking your head now and thinking what a dick, but in my defence, I was only 18 years old and yes, extremely naïve.

A couple of days later I got called back into the office and the boss gave me a packing list and told me to be ready in a few days' time. He said I was to be by the helipad at 12 noon, but to be prepared to wait as the helicopter would be heavily tasked and could well be delayed.

I enthusiastically started preparing. I had to go to the armoury and sign out a GPMG, then I had to go to the ammunition store and sign out a thousand rounds of ammunition for it, not thinking to ask why I would need a GPMG and thousand rounds on a building site. Then I had to take my personal weapon and sign out another hundred rounds for that, two smoke grenades, one chermoulie, enough personal clothing to last a month, several other bits of kit that I can't remember, a builder's hard hat and a hi-vis vest. I was told to pack my stuff into two holdalls and my bergen and be at the helipad at the right time with all this kit.

So I am at the helipad on time in full combats, hi vis vest, a bright yellow hard hat on my head and the GPMG butt resting on the ground.

Two hours later it started to rain.

Three hours in, it started to clear up a bit.

The bastards left me there for four and a half hours waiting for a non-existent helicopter that was never going to turn up. From that moment on my nickname was Trooper. (In the SAS a private is called a trooper.)

Simon (Trooper) Pickford. 1st Battalion Royal Green Jackets.

Are we made by the military, or do we join because we are like that anyway?

In 2004 a friend of mine called Ben worked for a marquee company that did weddings etc. Ben was a social hand grenade before and during his time in the army and would take loans out and just blow the money on alcohol and clothes with no idea how it was going to be paid back. He once booked a hiking trip exploring the Everest base camps which was paid for with a loan.

Ben's girlfriend Jane couldn't go with him to Everest because of the short notice, so they had an argument resulting in Ben saying he was going alone. Jane said "Well if you go, I won't be here when you get back." Ben went for three weeks or so and Jane was still at home when he got back. They're married now. Ha ha!

Anyway, back to Ben working for a marquee company. The company was hired to put up a marquee that was to be attached to a hotel in Somerset for the wedding of the England cricketer Xxxxx Xxxxxxxxxx which was also to be filmed. *(He did supply the name; I just don't want to get sued – Jonno DP).* They set up the marquee and got all the kit down there, hiring a generator for heating and power. Ben and the others from the company were suited and booted during the event, just basically there on standby in case something went wrong.

Well something did go wrong! The generator went down and there were no lights or heating in the marquee, so Ben's boss phoned the hire company and got a replacement on the way. He also ran some extension leads from the hotel so there was some, albeit reduced, light for the hour it was going to take for a new generator to arrive. He then sent Ben outside in the rain in his best suit to see if he could fix the failed gennie. Whilst up to his armpits in wet generator two men of the groom's party came out and asked Ben to come in because the groom wanted to see him. A bit puzzled, dripping wet, freezing cold and with an oily suit Ben went inside. Xxxxxxxxxx basically blamed Ben for the generator issues much to the amusement of the nearby guests. Ben tried to reason with him saying it's an engine, and things like this happen, and tried to persuade him all that was being done to resolve the problem. Xxxxxxxxxx was still not happy and chimed his glass with a knife. Once he had everyone's attention he announced to his guests that he was sorry for the situation and that Ben was to blame for everything that had happened. Ben got pretty pissed off about this and loudly suggested Xxxxxxxxxx come outside, "To talk about it". The two blokes who had spoken to Ben outside stepped in and said "Do you know who you're speaking to?" Ben knew who he was speaking to alright, and wasn't fazed a bit. He then loudly announced to the open-mouthed guests that he would, "Take these two outside one by one and knock them on their arses, then I'll have the groom". It's fair to say it was getting a bit heated and Ben's boss was trying to get through the guests to Ben and calm things down. Ben's still offering these guys out for a square go and the recently married Mrs Xxxxxxxxxx started crying. Cool as you like, Ben huffed and said, "For fuck's sake, as if I haven't got enough to do, I've got to shut her up as well".

Ben was eventually spoken to by his boss and it was all calmed down before any fighting started. Needless to say, he wasn't working for them for long afterwards and he soon joined the army. We would always have a laugh about it when we saw Xxxxx Xxxxxxxxxx on sky sports cricket and imagined a big deleted scene from his wedding video.

Michael Kettrick

I thought *you* had checked it....

Like most people would, I had a lovely time blowing things up when I was in the Royal Engineers, and it's surprising how relaxed you can get when dealing with explosives, sometimes perhaps a bit too relaxed. One day in the mid 80's we were sent out to Charlie Crossing on Salisbury plain to do a simulated artillery barrage on the river bank. We started laying it out and planned to detonate from the end of the bridge on the opposite bank, but we were a couple of metres short on detcord for the ring main. No problem, we sent the newbie back and after a bit he rocks up with a full reel of detcord, and we completed it.
After a bit some blokes from 3 Para come around the corner behind us giving it large with a gimpy mounted in the back of their rover, badges over their left ear, God's gift to soldiering. My Troopy hastily rolled the reel of detcord out of the way under the bridge said, "Watch this!" and set off the simulated artillery barrage.
Here's a handy tip for the next time you lay out a ring main from a reel of detcord (especially a full roll). Disconnect the detcord from the reel before you detonate....
We didn't.
The bridge went three feet straight up in the air and came back down intact. No casualties, and we gained a Para beret trophy for the mess.

Chris Delahorne, Royal Engineers.

"I don't know what effect these men will have on the enemy, but by god they terrify me."

The Duke of Wellington discussing British soldiers at the battle of Waterloo.

A social coup

In the summer of 1985, I was again in HMS Vernon waiting for a course to start and got nabbed for guard duty on a Friday. On the guard I was 'Pier Head Quartermaster,' which is the Navy term for the Guard Commander.
That Friday evening it was the HMS Vernon Summer Ball, a cocktail party for the officers and their partners. (Known to us commoners as a 'cock and arse' party, Cock = Cock and Tail = Arse.) A chance for all officers to drink, party and brown nose anyone senior…
At that ball there were two very junior officers that were doing a Mine Countermeasure Diving Officer course before joining the Minesweeper Squadron. Whilst they were out for a few drinks the night before the ball they happened to enter a hotel on Southsea common where none other than Oliver Reid, the legendary actor, and even more legendary drinker, was holding court. After a few drinks they invited him to the Summer Ball the next night. The officers were delighted at their luck and knew that this would give them a wad of brownie points and get them noticed! Such a social coup!
On the Friday the whole of the gate staff were on duty due to the extra traffic and extra security needed. At about 2000 hours the two junior officers were at the main gate to meet their esteemed guest who arrived in a limousine and was dressed in full highland regalia. Kilt, jacket, dagger in the socks the whole lot. He also had a beautiful young lady with him, who turned out to be his PA. He had obviously had a few to drink beforehand and the two officers escorted the unsteady Ollie to the ball. About thirty minutes later the guests of honour, Flag Officer Portsmouth, Rear Admiral Warsop and his wife turned up.

At about 2215 we were called to the wardroom lawn to escort a guest off the establishment. On arriving the guest turned out to be the legendary Ollie, who by this time was as pissed as a fart. We escorted him and his PA back to the main gate, and awaited his limo. By this time he was inviting us all back to his hotel for a drink but as we were on duty we obviously couldn't, so it was arranged for us to meet him in the bar tomorrow afternoon for a free piss up.

It was only after he had left that we found out what had happened. He had been introduced to the Admiral and his wife, and during the conversation taken his cock out and pissed over their feet without even breaking the conversation. We eagerly went to the hotel the next day, only to find he had left that morning without even leaving a drink behind the bar. The two officers who thought they were so clever inviting a 'Movie Star' to the ball were reprimanded and warned of their future conduct during their stay in HMS Vernon.

Dinga Bell Royal Navy 1973-1987.

A game of conquerors

The Centurion was everybody's favourite tank, and it was big, weighing in at around fifty tons. But in the late 1950s the Russians produced an even bigger tank and Britain responded with the Conqueror which was sixty-two tons and had a massive 120mm gun. In Hohne the 4th Hussars got their first three under cover of darkness one evening. Despite the secrecy there were three SOXMIS cars outside the back gate taking photos. Some quick thinker got fast drying bitumen paint and had the number plates on the tanks and the Antar tank transporters all painted out. Then with whitewash (for painting rocks normally!) different registration numbers were put on. They then drove out of the front gate, around the camp and back in the through the rear gates. That was repeated four times so the Russians must have used up a lot of film!

At the time I was REME attached to C squadron and was commanding the armoured recovery vehicle (ARV). Later in BAOR not damaging the locals fields and property became such an issue that some exercises were stopped because the money being paid out in compensation was getting too high. Not so in my day! Our Squadron Leader used to enjoy getting all the squadron in a line abreast in open country. He would look for some unsuspecting German farmer ploughing his field, declare him an enemy machine gun position and promise a crate of beer to the first vehicle to capture him (No. Not orange handbags! You are giving away your nig status there. It was Lunaburger Stubbies in the good old days, and 24 to a crate!). Well, of course, the ARV does not have a big gun or a turret to carry, and is therefore lighter, and faster than the tanks so we always won. I'm pretty sure that he realised why, but I think that he just enjoyed the hunt.

Ron Allen REME

Oi, you skinhead over there...

I did my basic training at depot in April 93 and joined A company of the 1st Battalion RGJ in October 93 just in time to fly out of Brize Norton to go to Cyprus. Hooray! Sunshine!

In July 1998 we were in Canada and me and my mate Rob Blundell had been on the piss in a town called Wainwright which was near the camp we were staying in. Rob was a bit of a nutter, in fact he was a lot of a nutter and he had a broad Lancashire accent that always made me laugh. His accent got stronger when he was drunk or wound up, which made him even harder not to laugh at. Mind you, I am from the North East and he thought I sounded funny too. One of his typical exploits was when we were sharing bunk beds (me on the bottom bunk, him on the top) and we'd been out pissing it up the night before. I woke up and wiped my hand across the springs above my head and thought 'Must have been cold last night, there's loads of condensation on here.' As I was thinking this my Rob popped his head over the side of the bunk (eyes, bloodshot, hangover for the use of) and said "I've pissed the bed. It must be the altitude or something". Cheers Rob.

Our acting OC in Canada was a great big Canadian bloke called Captain Anderson who had been attached to us from the Canadian army and came from the hilariously named Princess Patricia's Light Infantry Regiment. He looked pretty surf dude, long fluffy blonde hair and a great big droopy moustache.

About two weeks before he was due to go back we had a leaving do for him at the platoon lines, and were told there would be beers waiting for each of us. Lovely. Rob and I were still half pissed from the night before. Ah well, hair of the dog and all that.

After a bit Canadian Captain Anderson sees one of the full screws getting a haircut with an electric razor and says "I've never seen anything like that before, could you give me a haircut as well?" Everybody looked at each other, wondering what he was going to do, but the corporal just shrugged his shoulders and said, "Yeah if you want me to. Are you allowed to do this?"

Captain Anderson just said "I'm the OC. I can do what the hell I want".

Before he started, Rob, who was in a mood for some reason and now several beers closer to shitfaced, grabbed the electric razor and said, "Here give them to me, let me do it!"

The OC went along with this but asked him to put it on the longest setting, which Rob did, and off he buzzed.

To this day, I don't know why I did it, but about thirty seconds after this I ran over and said "Hey, why don't you let me have a go!" I don't know why I did this either, but I flipped the spacer off it, so there was no grading on it at all, and I was basically just shaving his head! I remember saying "Eee man, the lasses are gonna love you like. Especially your missus when you get home sir!"

I looked up and my Platoon Sergeant had a bottle and his hand and a shocked look on his face. He muttered "Fuck this, I'm getting out of here". After he went the other sergeants noticed what was happening and took off as well.

At a point past way too late, the platoon commander noticed what was going on and came across, gave the OC a bottle of beer and said in his very posh voice, "I don't think you're quite getting the haircut you asked for sir." Without saying a word the OC stood up and looked in the mirror and his mouth fell open. I swear to God he looked like a blonde Mick Miller.

He just breathed, "What the fuck!" and sat back down.

I asked him brightly, "Would you like me to finish it?"

He growled, "JUST FINISH IT!"

The stand-up comic Mick Miller

The OC (Artists impression)

Rob, who was well away by now, tried to grab the clippers off me shouting, "Ere, shave 'is tash off as well!!"
I fended Rob off and tried to cheer the OC up by saying that the bit I shaved will be covered by his beret. But in a hoarse voice he repeated that I should just finish it, so I just shaved the lot off. After I was done, and I, and

everyone else, had stopped laughing I started thinking, "Oh what the fuck have I done?"

Rob giggled and said, "They're gonna fucking kill you mate!"

So I suggested we shave her own heads so then it doesn't look like we've done it out of malice. Rob agreed this might help, so I shaved his bonce, and he shaved mine, then off we went up to the corporals' mess where the proper leaving do for the OC was being held. It wasn't long before the RSM grabbed us and said, "You two cunts like haircuts don't you? Just fucking wait until you see me in the morning".

As if we weren't in enough trouble, while the OC was giving his leaving speech, a very pissed Rob kept shouting out "Skinhead, skinhead, he's a fucking skinheeeeeeeeed".

The next morning a mate of mine on the Provost staff walked past us and said we were wanted in the guardroom by the Provost Sergeant, but we should stay well clear if we had any sense.

All innocence, I asked "What are we getting done for now? We've done nowt us!"

He roared with laughter and said "Are you fucking kidding? The whole battalion knows what you two did to the Canadian OC. It's being described as an 'exotic' haircut and the CO is doing his fucking nut. I suggest you fuck off quick, back to the Platoon lines and hide."

We asked if he knew any more about what was going on and he said that the RSM and the Provost Sergeant had spent the morning in the guardroom *combing* through Queen's regulations to find *something* to charge us with. I asked if he meant we were going to be punished for our exotic haircuts, or for doing it to the OC. He laughed again, and said he had been listening to them all morning going around in circles. They were just aching to jail us for what we did to the OC, but as he agreed to let someone cut his hair they can't do us for it. Worse for them but good for us, the OC can't very well punish us for looking like cunts with a stupid haircut when he's got one as well! My RP mate then told us "Besides, the CO can't punish you unless it's referred to him from the OC and he is refusing to do it! I tell you what though, you so much as fart on parade and they will give you 6 months in Colchester!"

To be honest, fully sober I felt a bit sorry for the OC. He had, apparently, spent all morning with the CO 'explaining himself'. The full story came out in the end. The CO tried to persuade the OC to get us done for assault but the OC wouldn't have it so the CO made him make a contribution to the officers' mess. I genuinely did feel bad, it was probably the worst and most expensive haircut he ever had, but I would have loved to have been a fly on the wall when he got home to his missus.

They never did find anything in Queens regs to punish us with, but we were marked men alright, and the RSM bided his time. A couple of weeks later me and Rob were downtown waiting for a pizza in a local takeaway. Because the pizza took longer than the guy said, we were back to camp late, getting in at 12:50 not the ordered time of 12:30. (We had the nickname the Cinderella Battalion because we weren't allowed out after 12:30.) Now in those days if you were charged you could expect about a week's delay before you were marched in front of your OC. Not this time. At 0730 the RSM bounded into the cookhouse while we were eating breakfast and said in a loud and happy voice, "Rifleman Martin, Rifleman Blundell, what fucking time did you get in last night?"

"12:50." I said, "You see sir, there was a pizza…."

The RSM wasn't even listening. "YES!!!" he roared, "TEN TO FUCKING ONE! I'VE GOT YOU CUNTS NOW!!"

By nine *that morning* we were in front of the OC and he deemed it too serious an offence for him to deal with. (Get the feeling they were after us?) By lunchtime we were in front of the CO getting a £150 fine each. Now as I said Rob's broad Lancashire accent made me giggle and as he was arguing about the unfairness I kept saying to myself over and over again 'Just don't laugh'. When we were marched out of the CO's office and into the RSM's he was absolutely raging because he had wanted us jailed. He absolutely let fly us, I swear the windows were rattling, he was literally foaming at the mouth, "ITS ALWAYS FUCKUING YOU TWO ISNT IT?? WHETHER IT'S SHAVING HEADS OR BREAKING WINDOWS, YES, I KNOW IT WAS YOU TWO!! I JUST CAN'T PROVE IT YET!!" (He was wrong there, it wasn't us, we *were* there when the extinguisher went through the window, I just cut my hand on the broken glass.)

He broke into my distraction, "OR IT'S BEING LATE BACK IN WHEN YOU FUCKING KNOW YOU FUCKING SHOULDN'T BE..." Veins were popping out of his head, they were popping out of his throat and I was trying very hard not to laugh out of sheer nervousness. The only way I stopped myself laughing while he was raging away was by watching these huge throbbing veins and thinking 'When he has a heart attack, what do we do? Should we just fuck off or should we tell someone?' He defo wasn't getting mouth to mouth.

Simon Martin, 1st Battalion Royal Green Jackets.

Thanks for your help Dad

I had a happy childhood growing up in a close community outside Barker Barracks in Paderborn. I attended Bishops Park School, which was my first military infant school, and even then we had homework. One night I had to do some handwriting exercises and I was really struggling. My Dad decided he would do my homework for me as he was convinced the teacher was picking on me.

The thing about us at the time was that we were one of the few mixed race families in the army. My mum is half Asian and was probably the best cook on the whole of Memel Strasse. Every weekend she'd be making a curry and me and my sister were forever going from house to house delivering plates of it to 'Aunts and Uncles'. That was the beauty of the 70s and 80s in Germany, you were one big family. My dad was forever bringing squaddies to ours at Christmas if they couldn't go home to their family.

Even though our blood family were in England, our everyday family were with us everywhere we got posted. When I meet up with my mum and dad's old friends, even now, I'm greeted as family.

Anyway, I took the homework assignment in and got told to do it again as it wasn't good enough. That was all my Dad needed to hear to convince himself that he had been right in his conviction that I was being picked on. He stormed up to the school and verbally laid into my teacher, giving him a right earful. A few days later when things had quietened down I came home from school to a clip round the ear and a bollocking from my old man.

Apparently teachers, although civilian employees, had honorary officer rank, and mine had reported my Dad to the BSM who duly put him on guard duty for a month.

How I got the blame as a 6 year old I'll never know...

Chris Dorney, Son of Mick Dorney J (Sidi Rezegh) Battery

(Editor's note; I actually knew Mick Dorney. He was one of those amiable lunatics that the army seemed full of at the time and would do things just because it amused him, which made him sought after company. One of his favourites was to bark like a small dog in crowded areas and then "Shush" the concealed pooch and watch people try and find it. Another, demonstrated to me shortly after I was posted in, was his fake German. He gave me a lift into town to open a bank account at the Sparkasse. At the time I spoke no German and was impressed by his ability to rattle away fluently (or so I thought). He was in fact just making German sounding noises to German people who were too polite to say the German equivalent of "What the fuck are you on about?" I finally twigged when we were walking past the Town Hall and Mick had his arm around the shoulders a middle aged German bloke he was having a prolonged conversation with.

I caught the words "Sucka meina cocka ja?"

"Ach, ja... ja... "responded the polite gent.

They don't make them like that anymore – Jonno DP)

"We all know the Navy is never wrong, but in this case, it was a little weak on being right."

Wendell Mayes

HMS Euryalus. Port Stanley Harbour, Falklands, 1986

We had been down south on patrol for five months during the British summer, which is the Falklands islands' winter if you didn't know, and were at a buoy in Stanley harbour awaiting our relief, HMS Dunbarton Castle, which was due to arrive the next day.

It was freezing, blowy and snow had been forecast for later on in the day. To my surprise I was told to lower the sea boat and take a painting party to paint the ship's side which hadn't been touched for over a month. I said to the officer who had ordered this fun activity that the weather wasn't cooperating, but he told us to get on with it anyway. We started painting and it started to snow. Then it started to snow more heavily. In five minutes it was a complete white out, and I mean 'not being able to see a hand in front of your face' white out. We told the officer that we were now painting in braille, but we were told to carry on as it would soon pass.

After a while, teeth chattering and desperate, I told the officer that the paint the Navy used had a rubberised finish and was only meant to be used on a dry surface or it won't bond properly. It was true. If this paint came off, it tended to come off in big sheets. I think he was tired of our protests by then and angrily told us to shut up and get on with it. After about half an hour, with the boat nearly full of snow, he either come to his senses, or it was the end of his turn at being a shit, and we were brought back on board freezing cold, and soaked through. The weather didn't change so we couldn't paint anymore and we all hoped we had done enough. The next morning we were relieved by Dunbarton Castle and sailed some two hours later.

The next day we carried out our last replenishment at sea with a Royal Fleet Auxiliary ship before heading north back to the U.K. Whilst we were doing this replenishment the crew watched two forty metre long sheets of shipside grey paint peel off the side and float away. Forty metres, which is a navy record I believe...

Dinga Bell Royal Navy 1973-1987.

Operation Agricola. Kosovo.

Back in June 1999 under the command of NATO and on behalf of Her Majesty's armed forces and the government, 24 Airmobile deployed one of its companies to bolster the numbers of 1st Battalion, The Royal Irish. It was my company. C company of the 1st Battalion Royal Gloucestershire, Berkshire, and Wiltshire Regiment. (The regiment's nickname was the M4's after the motorway.) We went in under the deployed name of Imjin Company, so as not to cause confusion between any other C company in the Brigade.

Imjin is not a name taken lightly within our regiment, as our predecessors were famous for their astounding bravery during the battle of Hill 235 on the nights of April 23rd and 24th 1951 during the battle of the Imjin river. This remarkable courage and tenacity at holding off the enemy whilst outnumbered 10,000 to 600 earned the regiment the Presidential Unit Citation (or Distinguished Unit Citation as it was known back then) from the American president Harry S. Truman.

Fast forward to Kosovo, June 1999. Boots already on the ground and routine patrols in place as we slowly advanced forward with the intent of pushing any pockets of remaining resistance out of the area as NATO moved on towards Pristina, the capital of Kosovo. One of Imjin company's tasks was to go firm and hold a village called Staro Gracko.

Our mission was to deter any more attacks on the few Serbians that remained in the village by other ethnic groups. There were only a few left, most had fled after attacks from ethnic Albanians who lived in the village and others from surrounding villages.

Whilst we were there, it would be safe to say that the soldiers of Imjin company grew very fond of these people who showed them nothing but kindness, respect and gratitude. There were even times when the soldiers who were not on stag would play five a side football with the younger villagers who came to see the platoon of young lads who were keeping them safe. Over time it all became pretty standard, football, banter and wind-ups. It was all the normal stuff you would expect and hearts and minds were exceptionally good.

Then an order came through ordering Imjin company out as the threat level was no longer considered high in the village. When the village elder found out that we were leaving he pleaded with us to stay and warned us that they would be attacked the moment that we left. It was up to a young officer to reassure him that everything would be fine, but the elder wasn't reassured and we all knew he was right.

We all pulled out that day and headed back to company HQ location and went on to QRF.

That same evening fourteen Serbian villagers in Staro Gracko who were tending to their crops were lined up and shot point blank in the head. Those that tried to run or get away on a tractor were shot in the back. Naturally, as we were on QRF, we were the first on the scene. I won't go into detail about what we saw on arrival or throughout that long and unpleasant night, but what I will tell you about is what happened the next day.

We were sent to set up a holding position in a school and, as we were in a mechanised role, we were using the good old Saxon APCs. We used the Saxon as a sentry point for the blokes to sit in whilst on stag. They would get into the commander's cupola and man the GPMG during their time up there. The next man on stag would knock on the back doors (which were obviously locked), the doors would be unlocked by the present sentry and a brief would be given at the commander's cupola. The brief was the usual stuff, amount of movement, pattern of life, absence of the normal or presence of the abnormal. Left of arc, axis, right of arc.

As you can imagine our morale was really low at that moment due to what had happened in that past 24 hours. Also, bear in mind that during our whole advance towards Pristina we had had no interest from the media whatsoever as that circus had been concentrating on the race between Russia and our paras to see who got to the airport first. Being filmed and admired is the paras' calling and this is their chance to prove to every other infantry regiment who mocks them that the British army still need paratroopers!

"Yeah, we're not going to rush and jump out of an aeroplane for this one, we're just going to drive our stripped-down Land Rovers and look alley the whole way."

WTAF?!!! Please tell me that you at least got there before the Russians?

"Ummm.... noo...."

You had one job to do, one fucking job....

Anyway, back to our shit fest. Now that there have been some murders in our location guess who thought they would grace us with a visit? CNN if you please! No interest when good things are happening, but as soon as there are some dead bodies, there they are! And they were not shy either! They were filming away, taking no account of the fact that people were identifying dead family members lying pulseless on the ground. This callous blonde thing decides to stand with her back to me in front of the Saxon that I was in whilst on stag. Still thinking about the events that had just happened I was slowly starting to get wound up about the lack of fucks given by this woman, just because she wanted to make a name for herself. Where was she when the villagers were playing football with us? Or giving us a sneaky couple of shots of slivo when we were out on foot patrol? Nowhere, because nice things, kind things, lovely things don't make the news.

Well, I couldn't handle it anymore so I did something that I think any young infantryman would do, or at least be tempted to do, in that situation. I picked up a weapon. I scoped the target in front of me, I took into consideration the wind direction and I judged the distance to my target using the halving method. I slowly opened the driver's hatch to be closer to the target, I was careful and made sure that it didn't creak. I think that the sun must have reflected off the driver's hatch as I slowly lifted it up, because although the CNN reporter was stood with her back to me, both her cameraman and sound man, who were standing either side of her, watched me emerge through the drivers' hatch. He looked at me in astonishment as I carefully raised my most cherished possession whilst out in Kosovo. Yes, that's right bitches, I had my wife send out a full-size pump action water gun. And boy did I plan to use it. This was no cheapo water rifle. This was an all singing, all dancing, keep your finger on the trigger for continuous firing, state of the art, choice of weaponry, and this reporter was going to get some. As I raised it I noticed the cameraman had a wry smile on his face as he alerted the sound man to my being in a firing position. I thought to myself 'Fuck! The soundman is going to bubble me. My position is compromised, and I'll have to abort.'

But to my surprise the soundman did exactly the same as the cameraman and looked away from me with a wry smile. On reflection I suppose this is understandable. If I hated the bitch in five minutes, I can make a shrewd guess at the opinion of people who had spent weeks in her company. All this was happening as the reporter was broadcasting live, and in dialogue with someone back in the USA. These two men had practically given me the green light and I was not going to wait a moment longer. I gently squeezed the trigger. The water overshot to the right. I kept the stream of water flowing constantly adjusting my aim as if I were tracking on a Milan firing post, tracking left, tracking, tracking, tracking good strike!!!! As I hit my target on the head and kept it there for what seemed like an age, I heard her voice go from a very composed journalistic reporters tone to the distressed shriek of a shocked stuck up snob. Then as if an alarm had gone off, I was suddenly brought back to my senses and realised that if I don't stop and go for cover, she would see that it was me. So, I dropped back down, shut the drivers hatch and was going to go back to the commander's cupola but heard the back door being knocked. I checked my watch, and would you believe it? It was the end of my stag.

I opened the back doors up for my mate Shep who was taking over. He asked me if anything had changed on the brief to which I answered, "No mate, still all the same as last time".

He nodded, closed the back doors and climbed in to the commander's cupola, expecting a quiet stag. As his head poked up through the cupola, he was met by an incredibly angry blonde CNN reporter who was gave poor old Shep both barrels. Private Shepperd's face was an absolute corker. He had no clue about what this woman was on about. This was much to the amusement of the rest of the platoon who witnessed the whole thing and just fell about laughing. As I walked off with tears in my eyes, I wasn't sure if it was from laughing or from what had happened the night before. Either way I could hear her calling him all the names under the sun. Even at a distance I could still hear her bawling,

"CALL YOURSELF A PROFFESSIONAL SOLDIER???"

"It wasn't..."

YOU SHOULD BE ASHAMED OF YOURSELF!!!

"But I..."

HERE I AM GOING LIVE ON TV TO REPORT ON THESE TRAGIC EVENTS AND ALL YOU CAN DO IS SPRAY WATER ON ME!! DO YOU THINK YOU ARE FUNNY???

"No, but listen..."

OH YEAH, LOOK AT ALL YOUR FRIENDS LAUGHING, REAL HEROES HERE!!!

At this point I heard Shep address me, shouting, "JP YOU PRICK!!"

175

Blondie continued, "YOU'RE ALL IMMATURE AND NEED TO GROW UP!!"

The journo bitch then calmed herself and said to Shep in an icy tone, "People have just been killed and you're all laughing, well it's no laughing matter. You are being very unprofessional".

I think that young lady couldn't have said it any better, but I wish she had stopped and had taken a look at herself and realised that she was the one that was unprofessional. Or maybe I mean lacking in humanity. Fourteen human beings had been murdered, and those very same soldiers that she described as unprofessional were the ones who had to clear the ripped bodies of those poor souls from that field.

RIP to the 14 souls of the Bloody Harvest Massacre.

John Parry, C Company, 1st Battalion Royal Gloucestershire, Berkshire, and Wiltshire Regiment.

Idyllic Camping on the riverbank

Our lives had got a bit predictable. Apart from going to work each day we were just drinking in the evenings and weekends, so we (me and other female military staff) decided we needed a change. We decided to go camping on the picturesque river Havel and drink there instead! The Havel is a pretty river that runs through Berlin and broadens out in many places. Perfect! We were all waiting for pay day and when it arrived we took the money we had all put in the kitty and bought booze, purloined a few ration packs and headed for the Havel. We found a lovely secluded area with a sandy beach where we could pitch our tents and drink the sun under the horizon. We lit a bonfire on the beach, had plenty of booze and food, and after a long and cheery night we went to bed.

At about two in the morning I was awakened by grunting. I nudged my friend irritably. Noisy cow.

I heard grunting again. Louder this time. I was about to nudge my friend harder when my blood turned to ice. The grunting was coming from outside of the tent. Then there was something pushing the side of the tent and I caught the stench of pig shit. Multiple grunts. Fucking hell! I realised with a rush of fear that we were surrounded by wild boar. If you are thinking 'So what? It's only a hairy pig isn't it?' The answer is no. The Central European boar has sharp teeth connected to powerful jaws and has been known to injure and occasionally kill people. I shouted to my mates to wake them up and told them that there was wild boar outside. After what you might call a lively debate and realising that the side of a tent was the only thing protecting us from the aforementioned sharp teeth, we took the only sensible option open to us, and panicked. We exited our tents like trains leaving a tunnel and with much yelling and screaming we ran in to the Havel. We figured the pigs could outrun us on land, but might be reluctant to enter the very cold Havel. The pigs did indeed seem to have more sense than us, and after they were done snuffling about looking for food and shitting everywhere they wandered off. The size of those tusks give me nightmares to this day. It's a good job they left when they did. We weren't exactly dressed for long stands in a cold river. Before much longer it would have been a choice between death by hypothermia and being bored to death. We hesitantly returned to dry land watching the treeline and with teeth chattering so much we could barely speak we re-entered our tents.

After a restless night where we woke up every time we heard, or thought we heard something, we all skipped breakfast and with many a glance in the direction the boar went we packed up and were on our way. On our way back to camp we drove past the Grunewald Forest which is the largest forest in Berlin. As we were driving along my mate nudged me and pointed into the trees. In the forest was a naked woman being chased by a naked man with a hard on and a dildo, and behind them a bloke dressed all in leather, with a perspiring cameraman bringing up the rear. (If you will forgive the expression.) It was like a Benny Hill sketch without clothes. Under normal circumstances this would have raised a lively reaction from us, but we were so knackered we barely raised an eyebrow. It was common to see sights such as these as pornographic films were often made in this area.

LCpl Linda Sykes (Rudkin)

"These people are ferocious barbarians who are barely kept in check by the firm discipline of the British Officer Core! In fact, the only reason the Northerners and Scots haven't eaten the soft officers from the Home Counties yet is because they think The Queen might not like it if they ate her officers. God help the world if we ever lose control of them."

Unknown American officer discussing British Infantry regiments.

Officers on the piss

In 1993 I was a craftsman in the LAD attached to an
artillery regiment in Dortmund, and me and my mates
were lemoned for waiting on at the officers' mess. We had
been out on the piss Friday night and were all in our pits at
about lunchtime, slowly surfacing when a sergeant came
into our six man room and announced, "I need six men to
wait on at the officers' mess for a do this evening." He
then pretended to notice that we were in the room. "Oh,
that's fucking handy," he pointed to us in turn, "One, two,
three, four, five." He pointed to the sixth person in the
room and said "Don't worry, not you!"
"Really?" said the lucky man.
"Just kidding!" said Sergeant Bastard. "Of course you
fucking are!" Right, get your kit on, you need to be in the
officers' mess in one hour."
We put on tracksuits and swore our way across to the
officers' mess and spent an unhappy afternoon putting
out tables, setting up marquees and wiping our bell ends
on spoons. It took all afternoon and after it was ready,
lucky us, we were told we had a couple of hours off before
we had to report back at 7pm in No2 dress to wait on the
tables doing silver service.
There was one thing out of the ordinary that happened
whilst we were setting up. Four senior officers came in
with large water rifles and hid them in the folds of the
tent, obviously planning some prank at the end of the
night. They were big ones too, holding a couple of litres
each. Well, the evening went as you would expect, we
turned up at 7 and watched a procession of smartly
uniformed Ruperts and their expensively dressed wives. As
is traditional for resentful underlings we plonked things

180

down as hard as we dared and were 'rewarded' at the end of the night with a polite ripple of applause from the officers and their ladies.

Thanks. That makes up for me losing my fucking weekend. Shortly after this the speeches started and the officers got the water rifles out of their hiding places and started to shoot the speakers, then each other and then anyone and everyone. This caused much mirth to all present and got squeals of laughter from the ladies being hit, even the one that got hit full in the face. It was all taken in good spirits and it only stopped when the rifles ran dry, and everyone was soaking wet. We didn't cop any of it. As soon as it started we legged it straight out of the marquee and were laughing our bollocks off at what we were watching unfold inside.

Why were we so amused? Well, what we knew and what they didn't was that after the four officers had hid the water rifles in the tent, we had removed them, drained them, pissed in them until they were full, and put them back.

Craftsman Keith.

Barking up the wrong stick

One time in 1980 we were on an FTX on Salisbury plain and we were putting in a platoon attack on an enemy position. It was the usual stuff, blanks being fired, smoke grenades popping and I saw an enemy trench right in front of me. I pulled out a thunderflash, struck it and threw it. So far, so ordinary, but then a small furry creature darted

181

past me, running like hell in the direction of the thunderflash.

Oh shit! "Here boy! Come here! Biscuits!"

BANG!!!

It turned out that the OC had brought his pet dog (a corgi if you are interested) on the exercise, and he loved to play fetch. (The corgi, not the OC.) Well, he used to love it. I couldn't see the dog after it ran past me, and I hoped the thunderflash had gone off before the dog got there. "Doggeeeee... good boy, come here, whistle whistle whistle......".

The platoon sergeant looked at me.

We both went into the wood, and well, let's just say the dog was too fast for his own good. By the time the CSM and the OC came over I had slipped away as far as I could in the vain hope that they wouldn't find out it was me. The OC was not a happy man. He found out who did it and wanted me charged, but I argued that the dog wasn't on a lead and it shouldn't have been there anyway. Maybe more out of fear of looking a dick than fairness towards me, the charge was quietly dropped. To be fair to him, the OC didn't hold it against me after he got over it but I did get the nickname 'Smudger the Dog slayer' for a bit though.

Chris 'Smudger' Smith. B Company Staffordshire Regiment.

Splish splash

After basic training I was posted to Herford in Germany to take up my post as a Catering Corps chef for the 9/12th Lancers stationed there. After a heavy night down town I stumbled in at about 3am. That I can remember, but everything else was told to me after the event.

Apparently, I arose from my pit and went to the toilets down the corridor. Except that instead of turning right out of my room I turned left. Whether I was sleepwalking or just pissed I don't know. Anyway, I am pissing away merrily when the guy I was pissing on woke up and said, "What the fuck are you doing Roger? The toilets are that way!!!" I said to him (apparently in an irritated voice) "Yes, I'm just having a piss, then I am going there!" Honestly, some people. When I finished I went back to my room and got into bed.

The SSM, Jimmy Hayden, called me into his office the next morning and didn't sound happy. Having no recollection of the previous night I went down wondering what on earth he wanted me for. He was a big guy, six foot two and solid, so I was a bit worried.

When I marched in he had an odd expression on his face, but spoke to me sternly. "Right! What happened last night?"

"Uhhhh......"

He coughed, put his hand over his mouth and said, "Come on!"

"Well.... Ummmm......"

"Did you piss on someone last night?"

"Uh?.... Well I was pretty hammered last night..." I heard a distinct giggle from him. This made me giggle too and he creased up laughing.

In the end I had to pay for a new mattress, wash his sheets, apologise, and live with the nickname 'Splash' for the rest of my time there. I reckon I got off lightly. Mind you, so did he. I pissed on the middle of his sleeping body, his head was closer to the door.

Roger 'Pelican' Kay. Army Catering Corps/RLC. Herford.

Things you thought you knew #4

No aircraft can intercept an American U2

The Lockheed U2 first entered service in 1957 and incredibly is still in service at the time of writing this in 2020! They were first used by the CIA to fly over the Soviet Union at 60,000 feet or more and photograph sensitive sites, an act of impudence that infuriated the Russians and they worked hard to find a way of bringing them down. They succeeded on the 1st of May 1960 when an attempt was made to fly a U2 from one side of the Soviet Union to the other. The Russians shot down the aircraft with an SA2 Guideline missile over Sverdlovsk and captured the pilot Gary Powers. All of this is well known, but after this incident the CIA continually upgraded the U2 in an attempt to make it able to fly higher than any missile, and maintain its ability to fly higher than any other aircraft, thus preventing its interception.
In September 1962 the CIA was keen to see if an English Electric Lighting (an aircraft that first flew in 1954) could intercept one of its vaunted U2's flying out of Upper Hayford in the UK at between 60,000 feet and 65,000 feet. To their astonishment, out of the 14 attempts the U2 was

intercepted 4 times. Realising their aircraft wasn't as safe as they thought, the CIA spent a fortune increasing the aircraft's capabilities further and by 1984, they were confident that once again the U2 was un-interceptable. Lieutenant Mike Hale of 11 squadron at RAF Binbrook carried out an attempted interception during a NATO exercise with the agreement of the CIA. The CIA was confident that the aging Lightning would stand no chance. Remember, it was thirty years old by now, and had not been substantially updated.

Turning almost vertically after leaving the runway Lieutenant Hale acquired the U2 at 66,000 feet, passed it, and topped out at an incredible 88,000 feet. He was over four miles *above* the U2! Oh, to have been a fly on the wall in the debrief of the U2 pilot!

If you want to see this amazing aircraft, it still exists. XR749 is in Scotland outside the gates of the Peterhead complex of Score UK, a company that services North Sea oil and gas rigs.

Researched and written by Jonno DP.

Traffic duty

One day on Exercise Lionheart in 1984 I'm dropped off at the junction of a forest track and a road with the instruction, "Any military traffic, you send it down this track."

So I dutifully direct all military traffic down the forest track. Bedfords, Ferrets, 432s, I think I even sent a Stally down there. It was a nice day and I was thinking that I was quite lucky that I had pulled this stag to enjoy a bit of peace and just wave the odd military vehicle down a track. After a bit my troop commander walks back up the track. An angry walk, and I wondered why he was walking instead of using his Land Rover. "What the fucking hell are you doing Sapper??"

"Sending all military traffic down the track..." I replied, baffled.

"I meant OUR unit you cunt! We can't fucking move down there..."

As you may have realised, the reason he had walked is that the small clearing earmarked for our detachment at the end of the track had long since been filled with military vehicles of all shapes and sizes, and they were now in a solid jam with only one way out, reverse a couple of kilometres. His lanny was deep in and there was no hope of getting around the solid mass of vehicles, hence he had to walk 3 kilometres out, enduring all the polite enquires from the rest of BAOR like, "What the fuck is going on?" and "Why has your fucking bloke sent us down here...... sir?"

It took hours to get 'em all back out again...

Chris Delahorne, Royal Engineers.

The bad penny

When I was in 3 Armoured Division Field Ambulance (3ADFA), Sennelager, we were doing an air portable exercise with RAF Chinooks that had partly American crews for reasons that I can't remember. We also had a new unit 2ic that I shall call Captain Bob, or as we used to call him, 'Bob the Born Leader'. He was a qualified paratrooper and had turned up, bursting with enthusiasm, at our unit which was filled with the army's biggest reprobates. (The RCT used to send their guys to us as a punishment posting.) You may think that the unit wasn't that rough because it was an Armoured Field Ambulance, but it really was. I didn't even speak to anybody for the first six months after I came out of basic training because I was so terrified of getting beaten up.

Anyway, we were very tired on this air portable exercise because there is a lot of humping and dumping of kit and we were very undermanned anyway. It was a real pain in the ass because we had to cover everything with camouflage nets as usual, but unlike other units we also had to put fuck off great red crosses on everything as well. So we're not in the best of moods when the super soldier second in command comes in wearing of all things, a home-made ghillie suit. A ghillie suit, if you don't know, is the outfit a sniper wears. I think he was doing this just in case any of us hadn't noticed the para wings sewn onto to his combat jackets, shirts, jumpers, and probably pyjamas. He started to lecture us about insufficient camouflage, no helmets, not wearing our Red Cross armbands, and that we could have all been sniped at. The thing that he made the biggest fuss about was that we weren't all wearing our Red Cross armbands. (Remember he's in a ghillie suit.) I remember thinking "What the fuck are you on you prick, you're a medic not the SAS".

Then he said "Come the next war, when it does happen," (note the 'when') "you could all get shot".

I had had enough and said, "Yes, and you'll be the first fucker shot, and it won't be by the enemy".

The whole room fell silent and I was whisked out of there sharpish by the sergeant major. As you can imagine, after that I didn't have the easiest of exercises, and when we got back to camp I was given seven days ROPs. The man really was a wannabe shit though. The CO was often away somewhere, as he was one of the main people doing the reorganisation of medical units in Germany, and as soon has his staff car was out of the gate Bob would have us running around Sennelager training area with bergens on. One time the CO returned from a three month trip and half the blokes were on crutches, light duties etc. I distinctly heard the CO say, "What the hell have you done to my unit?"

Some of the lads had even had T shirts made. On the front was a picture of a squaddie wearing an unfeasibly large bergen and the words underneath 'Bob the Born Leader's Commandos'. They got in the shit for wearing it during PT though.

After a few years I was posted and served in various places until in 1989 I was posted to 16 Field Ambulance, Bulford. On arrival the sergeant major marched me in to meet the commanding officer and fuck me, it was Captain Bob, now a Major. Before I had even finished saluting he laid into me with the words, "How the fuck did you get to full screw? You will never make Sergeant as long as I'm in charge of this unit, now get the fuck out of my office".

The mystified sergeant major marched me out and asked me what that was all about, so I explained. He said "Ha! You're in the shit here aren't you?"

I had a hard few months that turned into years. One day we were told manning and records were doing a tour of various units to explain to people how promotion boards and things like that are done. We were all told that we could, if we liked, request an interview with the officer doing the tour. I must have put in at least half a dozen requests and was turned down every time. When the guy came around we were all sat down in the gym waiting to be given the lecture by him. He did his bit about this is how such and such should be applied for, and how promotion boards work etc, and at the end of it he asked if there were any questions. Of course, my hand went straight up.

"Yes?" he said.

"Sir," I said, "can you tell me why, after I've requested an interview with you six times, I've been turned down for every one?"

At this point the Bob came to life and tried intervening and shutting me up, sitting me down and distracting the speaker but he was not having it. He said, "Yes of course, come and see me after the lecture." I went to speak to him and told him the whole story about Captain Bob. He listened to everything I said, picked up the phone, and got me a posting there and then to Germany as a sergeant. The only catch was that I had to be there on the 22nd of December. Not a problem, or so I thought.

Then the ambulance strike starts in 1989 and I am driving around Romford sorting out kit, wages and food etc for our ambulance teams who were working out of police stations to cover the duties of the civvy ones. Whilst doing this I kept ringing my boss reminding him that I was leaving soon, but it seemed Bob didn't want me escaping his clutches. My boss kept saying I couldn't go because they didn't have a replacement for me. Come the ACTUAL day I was supposed to be arriving in Germany, my wife handed the quarter over (immaculate, as she always left quarters), picked me up from the police station in Romford I was working out of, and we drove to Germany. Now it's his problem.

When I got to Germany there was a bit of a hoo-ha, but ultimately my new CO agreed that this shouldn't have happened. Somehow Bob managed to stick one more to me and we got a hefty cleaning bill for the quarter. But at least I wouldn't have to see him ever again.

A few months later in 1990, the Gulf War started and I was sent out with 14/20th Hussars (tankies) as part of their Armoured Ambulance. Two days before the war kicked off proper, I saw some sandy coloured Toyotas coming across the desert. They stopped near us and out steps Captain Bob, only now he is a full colonel. With him, the usual flunkies, Aide, driver, bodyguard, arse wiper. He catches sight of me and double takes.

"Oh fuck, it's you. Where's the fucking section sergeant?"

"I am the fucking section sergeant."

"Oh, right."

We then had a short conversation about did we have the right kit, and were we familiar with procedures in case of this and that, as you do.

Before he left, his driver approached me and a couple of the other lads and asked for some help with his satnav. Unlike the things you can get today ('today' is June 2020) these were clunky, unreliable and quite difficult to use. If I remember rightly you needed line of sight to five satellites for it to work. They were called Magellans and front line units like ours had been issued with them. Anyway, we had sussed them out a while back, and Bob's driver asked us if we could show him how to use it and particularly how to set waypoints. He needed this, as his job was driving the Colonel to points all over the place in a featureless desert to check on various field ambulance sections attached to front line units.

What an opportunity! We fucking programmed that satnav alright! We sent him all over the place, especially places where wheeled vehicles bogged down easily and there was poor radio communication. Several points were within range of Iraqi weapons, and one point we set was eight miles behind enemy lines.

I found out later that after 16 Field Ambulance he was never put in a position again where he commanded a unit and was side-lined into administrative posts. Apparently, my fall out with him was not the only one he had had, and stories had reached the ears of the people who made these decisions. And is case you are wondering, he didn't get killed or captured in Iraq despite everyone's best efforts.

Rob P 3ADFA Sennelager

A special ND

As a young bloke I went to Cambrai barracks in Catterick in 1988 to do my basic training. After you finished that you were sent off on your trade training, in my case a gunnery course, but I got chickenpox and they sent me home for two weeks. After I got back they said there were no gunnery courses that I could join, so I had to be sent to my regiment unqualified. On arrival I was put into 4th troop, I squadron, Queens Own Hussars and told we were to be doing a range day in about four weeks and I was going to be the gunner on callsign four-two. Realising I was untrained they condensed a seven week gunnery course into a one student three week course. Cutting corners with gunnery. Surely nothing can go wrong...

So come the range day, off we go. There is an exercise you do on the ranges where the tanks line up on the hard standing and you scan the ground in front of you. A target pops up, all the tanks have to find the target, lase it, and select the ammunition. The person in the tower then calls which callsign is to shoot. On this day, the person in the tower was captain Keogh, a Geordie that had risen through the ranks and whom everyone was terrified of. Up pops a target, I lase it, select HESH, and captain Keogh says, "Three two, yours"

BOOOOOOMMMMM! Went our main armament.

Hang on. Did he say three-two or four-two?

Oh fuck! We are four-two and he said three-two...

At the time there was a story circulating that a 9 millimetre round cost 3 pence and if you had an ND with one you got six months in Colchester nick. I started to calculate how long I would get for chucking a 120mm, £20,000 round down the range.

Captain Keogh called out, "Who was that?"

My commander, a fella called H. Allsworth, said, "Sorry sir, I think my gunner got a bit carried away".

"He WILL get fucking carried away if you don't sort him out and so will you."

To be fair, there was no comeback from this, but I don't know whether it was because they had condensed the gunnery course down to three weeks or because I hit the target, and quicker than the person who was actually meant to kill it!

Trooper Stuart Weston. Queens Own Hussars.

I wonder what this button does...

On Friday October the 12th 2018 at Florennes Air Base in the Walloon area of Southern Belgium, a Belgian air force mechanic working on an F16 fighter aircraft accidentally fired its M61A1 Vulcan cannon. This is a lively bit of kit. The Vulcan is an electrically driven, six-barrelled gatling gun which fires 20mm rounds at 6,000 rounds per minute. That is 100 rounds per *second*!

He did not have a lucky break. He hit another F16 which caught fire and exploded having recently been refuelled and made ready for a training sortie due to take place later that day. Another one, possibly two (depending on who you ask) aircraft also received minor damage. No one was killed, but two groundcrew who were stood near the front of the F16 when it fired were treated by medics for temporary deafness and probably shitty underpants. Belgium's air force has 60 F16's, sorry, my mistake, Belgium's air force has 59 F16's and vacancies for ground crew too I expect. After the accident the base commander Colonel Didier Polome suspended all flights whilst the incident was investigated. This was an expensive accident, F16's cost about 19 million dollars each.

A bad day at the office

The Belgian air force was unhappy with the Belgian newspaper De Standaard for an article taking the piss out of the air force for destroying one of its own aircraft. It makes you wonder if the mechanics now have an F16 shaped sticker on the side of their van, a bit like RAF pilots put stickers of shot-down ME109's on their spitfires during

WW2. The article is understandable though as the Belgian air force were reluctant to confirm or deny any facts. Later on, Colonel Polome and Jeroen Poesen, who was the Commander of Kleine-Brogel air base, said that maintaining a world class air force was a serious business and pilots and support crews had recently worked successfully as part of NATO missions in the Balkans, Afghanistan, Libya and the Middle East, but admitted it was a serious incident that must be fully investigated. The problem that the Belgian air force has now, apart from being an easy target for jokes, is that this reluctance to talk has inevitably fuelled rumours. One rumour is that it was sabotage. This seems unlikely. If a terrorist nutcase had done it they would have announced it to the world, and who else would have an interest in sabotage? Did the mechanic want to sabotage it for some reason? If so, why haven't they released his name and just said so?

The Belgian Aviation Safety Directorate is currently investigating the incident and was due to report in the spring of 2020. At the time of writing (Autumn 2020) no report has been made. With Covid 19 shutting many things down this is perhaps, understandable. But if you dig a bit deeper, some people (mostly Americans) who have worked on F16's are asking some awkward questions. For example;

"This accident is quite weird. Why was the technician working on an armed aircraft that close to the flight line? The Belgian air force has not said what type of inspection or work was being carried out. Obviously, it must have been a check that activated the gun, even though the aircraft was on the ground. The use of the onboard weapons (including the gun) is usually blocked by a fail-safe switch when the aircraft has the gear down with the purpose of preventing exactly this type of accident."

Or how about,

"In addition to the WOW safety interlock, which would have to be overridden, there should also be a safety pin (with flag) that the pilot or armourer would remove as the pilot performs his pre-flight walkround. Within the cockpit, the Master Armament control would have to be set to Live and the Gun would also have to be selected via the weapons selector (Gun, Missiles, Bombs etc). Also – why is an armed aircraft inside a hangar and electrically powered-up? There is a lot more to this story than has been divulged so far."

But then there is this,

"I was stationed in Florennes back in the mid 80's. While the Belgians are very nice people, their concept of OPSEC and flightline security was not the most stringent. We had a Local National Secretary showing recon photos that her husband had taken the day before for the Americans. They were supposed to be stamped SECRET but she was showing them to all the people she was working with. So this 'mechanic' may actually have been someone's spouse or child who wanted to see what their relative did at work and was sitting in the cockpit of a mission ready aircraft, and not one that had been safed for visitors."

But I think the last word goes to,

"Does the technician get credit for two kills? Three more and he'll be an Ace!"

Researched and written by Jonno DP.

Medic!!

We were on tour in Northern Ireland but I had to wait until after I was 18 to be allowed to go on patrol like everyone else. We had our first contact when we were walking in an extended line across the field. It was a single shot, then a burst of automatic and we had all hit the deck after the first shot, adrenaline pumping. We tried to identify the source of the shots and started to pepperpot towards where we thought it was. By the time we got to the place there was no one there. One of the guys had a quick look round for IEDs and things. Nothing. But in the near distance we could see a florist's van driving off at high speed so one of the guys opened up on it. Fortunately he missed, as the innocent woman inside it had also heard the burst of automatic fire and had decided to put her foot down to get away from it.

Then we realised one of our lads was missing. He was back in the field waving his arms around and shouting as he'd been pinged by the first bullet. Fortunately for him the bullet ricocheted off a nearby rock and had much less force when it hit him in the leg. Anyway, we sent Smurf, who was our medic, back to check on him and although he was in pain he wasn't badly wounded. Smurf was having a bit of a flap about this and got a syringe of morphine out, but out of sheer panic stuck it in his own leg. So now

instead of having one casualty we have two... Fortunately it was all helicopters there, so we got lifted out by a Crab Air Wessex helicopter.

It was a bit of an eventful time overall actually. Later on, someone in our patrol put a couple of rounds in a cow because, he claimed, "It jumped out on me from a bush." No one believed him.

Simon (Trooper) Pickford. 1st Battalion Royal Green Jackets.

How the other third live

There is a long history between the Army and the RAF that is not always polite. The Army thinks the RAF is over-privileged and pampered, and the RAF thinks the Army are a bunch of smelly ruffians, hence the nickname Pongos. (Where the Army goes, the pong goes.) I think I may have confirmed this prejudice in the eyes of the RAF when I visited one of their bases.

Sometime early in the 1980s I was detailed to drive a Bedford truck with a load of swingfire missiles to RAF Gutersloh to be flown out to Canada. Why my battery had to do it I don't know because I don't remember us having any Canada training on the horizon.

I got told about this just before we came back off exercise and complained that I would be getting out of one vehicle and straight into another without a chance to even have a shower or get changed. My protest was met with the usual level of sympathy that you can expect if you are a nineteen year old gunner, and the niggiest nig in the unit. For a reason I can't remember BSM Geordie Grant said he would do the armed escort for this trip, so when we returned to Barker Barracks in Paderborn I got out of an FV438 and climbed into the cab of a recently emptied Q's Bedford. We had only one stop, and that was the guardroom to sign out and collect live ammunition for my and the BSM's SLRs. Off we went, I think to Depot 90, to pick up the pallet of swingfire missiles that we were to deliver, then to RAF Gutersloh so Biggles and his mates could fly them to Canada.

The journey itself was pretty uneventful but I do remember BSM Grant telling me stories about being a military trainer in Rhodesia/Zimbabwe and how fucked up it all was, and how unrealistic the instructions were that the military had received from the political masters. Oh, same there then.

Anyway, we got to RAF Gutersloh and delivered the missiles. We were then told that we could go and have a meal at the cookhouse. Brilliant! I was fucking starving! I had been on compo for a fortnight! So I drove the BSM to the sergeants' mess or whatever the RAF call it and I was given directions towards the RAF other ranks cookhouse. I drove up the road that I've been directed to drive up, and all I could see was some offices, accommodation blocks, and an officers' mess of some sort. When I got to the end I turned around and drove back again checking more carefully this time. Once again all I could see was offices, some accommodation and an officers' mess. Thinking I must be on the wrong road completely I drove back to where I got the instructions outside the sergeants' mess.

The same person who had initially given instructions smiled the sort of smile you would give to a backward banjo playing cousin that's lost, and confirmed that I had been on the right road. Thinking I must look pretty stupid, I drove back to the road and looked much more carefully for the cookhouse this time. Accommodation...... offices...... officers' mess..... that IS an officers' mess isn't it?

Being hungry, irritated and running out of the time the BSM had allowed me to eat, I decided to ask a passing..., well not being familiar with RAF ranks I have no fucking idea what he was. When I asked where the OR's cookhouse was he pointed to the officers' mess that I'd driven past three times. I said thanks, and thought, 'Is the piss being taken here?' I mean, I could see inside this building and it had sofas. It had pot plants. Unlike army cookhouses it didn't look like a badly refurbished public toilet. Therefore it must be a Mess, unlike army cookhouses which are a mess.

So I walked in scanning the entire room carefully and the occupants, to a man, carefully scanned me. I had been on exercise in hot weather for two weeks and I hadn't cleaned myself more than had been sufficient to ward off the Troop Commander's anger, so I was probably smelling a bit spicy by this time and there were a few wrinkled noses as I walked in. A manky gunner in filthy boots and combats, an SLR over his shoulder and a magazine of live ammunition bulging his top pocket. I was expecting somebody to scream at me to fuck off out of their nice clean Officers' Mess, but it didn't happen.

Whether the people sat at the tables were the lowest of the low or an air vice-marshal, I had no clue, as I said I had

no idea what RAF ranks looked like. Shortly after entering, someone took pity on me and said, "You alright chum?"
I confirmed I was a twat by saying, "I'm looking for the OR's mess".
He frowned and said, "You're in it....."
I saw several people turn to their dining companions and say something like, "Yeah, defo army".
Having established that I was in the right building I approached the slop jockeys standing behind the food counter. Now, if you go to eat in an army cookhouse it can be a painful experience. One sausage too many and you'll feel your knuckles rapped with a metal ladle by a festering sloppo. So I approached the RAF sloppos with some caution, not really knowing what the rules were. I was aware I still had a lot of eyes on me, as a grotty soldier in my state and a bang bang with live bullets was not something that they saw every day in their posh restaurant. And I didn't know what would incur the sloppos wrath, so it must have looked slightly peculiar to anyone watching when I picked up a slice of bread and then slowly took one more burger than everybody else whilst watching the guy behind the counter. He just looked at me and smiled. He didn't even give the traditional greeting that an outsider would receive in our cookhouse i.e "Who the fuck are YOU!" He didn't belt me. He didn't shout. He didn't even call me names. It was an odd experience overall.
I only embarrassed myself once more when I went to get some coffee from a fancy looking machine. I stood there looking at it whilst a couple of guys waited patiently behind me.
"Where do you put the money in?" asked the shit-covered intruder.

The guy behind me shook his head, smiled, and said, "It's free"

As I walked away I heard him mutter to his mate "Fucking pongo's".

Fair one really.

Jonno DP. 3RHA.

I feel the need for speed

I had to admit it. Fun though it was being stationed in Berlin, the good times were starting to take their toll. Me and other female personnel would have some great nights out, more often than not booze fuelled and I decided that I had put on a bit of weight. It *might* have been from all the drinking. Let's face it. It WAS the drinking. My friend Tracy had heard of some amazing slimming pills that could be bought in the Apotheke in Friedrichstadt. She told me the slimming pills came in a green and black box and which shelf they were on. Off I trotted to the Apotheke and bingo, found the tablets, went back to camp and took two of them. My god! I couldn't keep still! I felt very alert, never seemed to get tired when doing something and felt quite excited about things. At first I didn't give it much thought, but I couldn't sleep, was hyper-vigilant and seemed to be talking more than I used to. I stuck at it, and continued to take them for a week and lost those extra few pounds. I decided that maybe I should stop when I found out that I had, in fact, been taking speed and that I was off my tits on the stuff.

LCpl Linda Sykes (Rudkin)

"Hangovers are temporary. Epic tales of drunken adventures last forever."

Anon

It's mine! It's mine!

We had been in the Falklands for a while when one night we 'borrowed' a Land Rover from the MT section and went into Port Stanley for a few drinks. Before we got to the first watering hole my mates Geordie Brad and Chris Wainwright dropped me at Errols, a big, bald and extremely effeminate barbers to get a haircut. I walked in and he span around with a huge happy smile on his face, "Oooh!!!" He said, apparently delighted at the prospect of having a military man in his proximity. "What can I do to YOU?"

A bit blindsided by this I blurted out, "**I JUST WANT ME HAIRCUT!**"

"Oooh lovely, take a seat!" I did.

He then locked the door and lowered the blinds. There is probably no need to explain how this made me feel. To be fair he did a good job of cutting my hair whilst I sat bolt upright, rigid in his chair. When he finished and without turning my back on him, I paid and left.

I joined my mates in Deanos then we went to the Globe, then back to Deanos as I knew the landlord there. He was an ex-army chef, Pete Parr I think his name was, and he used to keep bottles of apfelkorn (a type of schnapps) in the freezer for us, which we used to try to drink by the bucketful. They had a karaoke night on and we were all absolutely hammered. As you do, one of my mates put my name down for the Elvis version of Suspicious Minds so I got up, belted it out and sat back down. They do say that the secret of singing well is to relax, which isn't easy when you are singing in front of an audience. I can assure you that this problem is easily overcome with three quarters of a bottle of apfelkorn. In fact I was so relaxed, I nearly did a header off the stage several times. At the end of the night a winner of the karaoke had to be found and guess who minced up to the stage to choose the winner? Errol, the hairdresser.

Errol flounced about the stage for a bit and locking his eyes on me he oozed, "The winner is Mike from Mount Pleasant".

I don't know why he called me 'Mike from Mount Pleasant' rather than just 'Mike'. I have a sneaking suspicion his subconscious was at work and he was thinking it would be 'Pleasant to Mount Mike'. Happily though, the prize was worth having, a case of twelve bottles of white wine.

So me and the lads, by now very relaxed indeed, drove back from Stanley to Mount Pleasant. Halfway back I asked the driver to stop as I needed a piss. The rest of the lads got out too and we all lined up on the edge of the track.

You know how when you are pissed, and you suddenly get an idea? Your brain then goes, "Thash a GOOD idea. In fack it's a BRILLYUNT idea. Ackshully, I have to do it NOW, its sho fucking GOOD!!!!"

The idea that I had was to get the sign that was about a hundred yards from me as a souvenir of the Falklands. The sign said 'MINES' and it was on the far edge of the minefield.

I bet one of the lads one of the bottles of wine that I could run across the minefield and bring it back before he could. You may have noticed the illogicality of this proposal. They were MY bottles of wine, I had won them. In fact, just to add spice to the bet I would do it naked! Not wanting to be outdone my mate agreed and on the executive word of command we both started stripping off, and I belted over the minefield, pulled up the sign and belted back. When I got back I found my mates laughing like fuck and I was handed a bottle of my own wine as a prize. By the way, my rival in the race only pretended to start stripping off, got redressed, and watched my sporting attempt at suicide without moving more than three feet from the Land Rover. Funny thing, after I got back and got dressed I couldn't find me undercrackers, I remember kicking them off with my foot, I reckon they are still in that minefield. If anyone finds them, I would like them back. I still have the sign!

SAC Mike 'Bert' Eisinger. RAF.

(Editor's note, there were several minefields laid by the Argentinians during the war and they would have been dangerous to clear, so the land was just abandoned. You might think this strange if you live in crowded Europe, or even more crowded Britain, but the Falklands has roughly the same area as Cornwall, Devon and Somerset combined with a population of less than 3,000 people. The minefields became nature reserves for penguins, and they say penguins can't fly!)

Tanks very much

I went to Detmold as a very young craftsman and was put
to work in a large ex-Luftwaffe hangar used by 4
Armoured Workshops for tank repairs. I was so new to the
job and had so little experience and training that I hadn't
even been taught how to drive a car! One day I was told
by the sergeant Major, making one assumption too many I
think, to get the tank I was working on out of the hangar
as the space was needed for something else. Always one
to obey an order without question I jumped in and started
it up, getting my daft as a brush oppo to guide me out of
the hangar and park the tank outside. Now, tanks are big
heavy vehicles obviously, and sometimes things happen
that you might not notice...

I drove the tank out, parked it, shut the engine down and
dismounted. No problem. Then it was pointed out that the
gun barrel of the tank I had been driving had gone straight
through the hangar door (I had neither seen, nor heard
anything). In typical army fashion a large crowd soon
gathered as they always do to enjoy someone else's
misfortune and offer helpful tips like "You should be more
careful" and "Ha ha, you're really in the shit now". My
oppo had disappeared (thanks buddy) and I was left to
face the music alone.

Surprisingly the boss was good humoured about it and a
decision was made to remove the buckled plate and
replace it with a window as it was badly lit inside at that
point. No more was said about the incident even from the
WO2 who told me to move the tank. So for as long as I
was there, there was this big stretch of steel hangar doors
and one single, lonely window. If you look up Detmold
Glider Museum on the net you can still see the hangar

with new doors. The window is not there anymore, but there is still a hole in it as a testament to my tank driving skills.

Craftsman Derek Grater REME. 4 Armoured Workshops. Detmold. A long, long time ago.

Time for a quiet smoke...

We were in Crusader in 1980. Maybe it was Lionheart '84, I can't remember now, but I do remember we were on Sennelager ranges doing MSR's, and got some R&R. We went on the piss in Bielefeld. Why Bielefeld I can't remember either, it's miles from Sennelager and there were plenty of bars much closer. Whilst in Bielefeld we had a spot of bother with some lads from 10 Regiment RCT when I had a fight with some shit with a boxer's nose. I found out later he was in fact a very good heavyweight boxer. (10 Reg RCT were big on boxing.)
We were meant to be on the transport at 1am without fail, so at about 4am Davey Barras and me started wondering how we were going to get back to Sennelager, which is about half an hour's drive away.
Left with no choice we took a taxi, but as we were going through Sennelager ranges the taxi driver told us how much it was going to cost, (a fortune) and I started arguing it was too much. He screeched to a halt and refused to take us any further unless we paid now. Things got a bit heated so I said to my mate we would walk the rest of the way. I threw a handful of ten mark notes at him, got out and told him to fuck off. As he sped away I realised that

my mate Davey was still asleep in the back seat and the driver hadn't realised.

Bollocks.

So I started walking down the range road in what I thought was more or less in the right direction. After a bit I heard some noise in some bushes off to the side of me. I looked at the long, long road stretching in front of me and thought fuck it, if there is a British unit here, I will go in, show my id card and maybe I can kip somewhere until the morning, or if they have a duty driver maybe I can even get a lift! I walked towards where I heard the noise and couldn't see anyone, but peering through the dark I eventually made out the wheel of a trailer, so I went over, sat on the wheel and got a fag out. In those days I had the habit of using Swan Vestas and striking them on the nearest rough surface. I found my matches and struck it on the wheel arch of the trailer I was sitting on. As I cupped my hands around the flame I noticed that there was some light being reflected from ABOVE me of all places. Still pissed, but curious, I looked up and saw above me a big shiny tube. Weird. I raised my match and saw that in front of me the tube came to a point. Very weird. I looked back and realised that the wheel I was sitting on had a pole coming out of it that was propping the tube up. What kind of trailer was this?? I looked behind me and saw wings, more wheels and the rest of a Harrier jump jet. You know when you are so pissed that you just stop, look, and think 'I know this isn't real, but I'm damned if I can work it out?' I sat there wondering for a bit and then noticed a bloke coming towards me. I opened my mouth to speak, got hit in the face by a rifle butt, and everything went black.

When I came to, I was in a guard room tied to a stretcher. Standing above me were two excited RAF officers talking in posh high-pitched voices. I started trying to explain the situation, but it wasn't helping because a) I have a very strong Geordie accent, b) I was talking very fast because I was worried I would get another rifle butt in the face, c) I was still quite pissed and d) I overheard them discussing the fact that I was a Russian spy. They turned their attention to me and told me to, "Shut up you commie, the Military Police are on their way!" This just made me gabble even more.

This went back and forth until a tired looking Scottish Sergeant from the RAF regiment stamped across and irritably said, "He's not a Russian. He's a fucking Geordie!!" It sounded like it was 50:50 whether he ended the sentence with 'Sir' or 'You assholes!!' He got control of himself and settled on "Sir."

Even better, they had been on the radio net saying they had caught a Russian spy sneaking around a Harrier jump jet and ordered an increase in the guards, so now there were dozens (maybe hundreds?) of RAF blokes no longer in their scratchers, but instead in a slit trench. Ha ha, you are welcome lads.

In the end they untied me from the stretcher and gave me some breakfast and first aid for the split on my head caused by the SLR butt. I told them I had to get back to my unit (it was daylight by now) but the Jock who had saved me from an over-excited RAF firing squad told me that my unit was sending a vehicle. The vehicle turned up and it was driven by my ASM.

Oh, fuck, no.

He just pointed to the back of the rover and said, "Fucking in".

There was a stony silence all the way back to my unit and when I got there I was under open arrest whilst on exercise, which is a new one.

I asked about Davey and was told the taxi driver had taken him to Bielefeld and dropped him at an RMP station. With the kindness and generosity of spirit that makes the RMP so popular with squaddies they hosed him down every half hour to keep him awake until he was picked up.

Craftsman Geordie Hands REME attached to 1BR Corps HQ.

"Being in a navy ship is like being in jail, with the chance of being drowned."

Samuel Johnson

Just a few beers won't do any harm

Batus 2003. I was a Lance Jack crewing the AVRE on the standard brigade exercises. When the exercise ended, we came in off the prairie and queued up for the washdown, but it was hardly moving. Because of foot and mouth disease there was lots of extra care that had to be taken and the washdown was going to literally take days, so we all left the vehicles until the next day and walked back to the accommodation for a shower and a decent bed. I was on a drinking ban for previous misdemeanours, so I decided I would have just a *few* beers. I had also lost my R&R for another misdemeanour. (I spent the night in some bird's bed and turned up a bit late. Well, very late to be honest.) Off I went with my mate determined to be sensible but one beer led to another, and another led to quite a few, and, well, I am sure you know how it is... By the small hours we had had many, many silver bullets in the Suffield bar we were absolutely ballbagged. As you probably know, alcohol tends to encourage projects that under more sober circumstances might be regarded as a bit much, and me and my pal decided it would be fun to have a little play with all those unlocked vehicles parked at the washdown. It was about one-ish and people with any sense were asleep.

The vehicles were parked probably best part of a mile away from the accommodation and bar area so we knew we wouldn't be heard. Great!

We staggered off to the washdown, got into an infantry 432 and started her up.

Wahey!

I roared off and was driving as fast as I could with my mate in the commander's hatch. We were having a fine old time racing in and out of the lines of vehicles. Until I slewed and completely levelled a portaloo. My mate cracked jokes about shit driving and laughing our asses off, away we went again. I misjudged another corner and clouted the barrel of an AS90 self-propelled artillery gun which is a bit more expensive than a plastic shithouse. We had a look at it, and it didn't look right. Oh well, someone will sort it out in the morning. Probably just a tap with a hammer back the other way. We thought we had better pack it in there though, so I turned the engine off and we fucked off to our beds.

The next morning we had breakfast and walked back to the washdown with a hazy recollection of…. OH MY FUCKING GOD!!!

It was like NCIS Canada… MP'S were swarming all over the place, taping everything up, keeping everyone away and trying to work out the crime scene. Nobody was ever any the wiser and we got away with it, fuck knows how. Our paw prints must have been all over the place. We dodged a huge bullet that night! If we had been caught it would have been Colchester and goodbye army for sure!

Ches and Griff. Royal Engineers.

REME can remove engines *fast*

In Volume one of We Were Cold Warriors there were several references to REME's FV434s. Before they came though, we had American International Half-tracks, with a high folding jib on the front. Mine was built in 1944 and still had the white stars visible under the green paint. They were for FRT work on Centurion and they were good. Fully enclosed, four fitted bunk beds, a plate that you could remove to get heating into the cab and enough space to replace the terrible US Army seats with something of your own choice. Mine had seats out of a Jaguar limousine and it had a top speed of around 60mph! I was clocked through a village one night at 62mph, but I convinced the copper that his equipment had to be faulty.

When Chieftains were issued to the armoured regiments we were re-equipped with FV434's and the good days were gone. I was then a fitters Troop Leader with 16/5 Lancers and I rode in an FV432, so at least I still had a bunk. My 434 crew were great guys, but a bit laid back and had allowed the 434 to get quite scruffy so I ordered it cleaned up. The guys got on with it cheerfully, but I got a bit concerned when they went under the vehicle and unscrewed the escape hatch and lowered it to the floor. This was a very heavy two foot by two foot square lump of armour plate which they took out to make hosing it through easier. I wasn't keen on this, but they had already done it, so I contented myself by saying that they were to be very sure to refit the hatch properly.

A few days later we left Fallingbostel to go on exercise. Whilst we were leaving camp I had been delayed slightly, so instead of being in my usual position I was at the very rear of the squadron with my 434 in front of me. As we were going along a German police Volkswagen Beetle had pulled out in front of me and was now unwisely driving only feet from the back of the 434. Without warning the armoured escape hatch fell out of the bottom of the 434 and bounced along the concrete. I watched in horror as the Beetle ran over it, it bounced up in the air three times as the plate rolled, then the plate tore the engine out in one lump, and left it sitting in a pool of oil. The quick removal of the engine also ripped the back axle off and what was left of the car belly flopped onto the road. Removing the engine was easy, but putting it back in may have been a bit harder!

Ron Allen REME

"They couldn't hit an elephant at this dist.."

Last words of Major General John Sedgwick at the Battle of Spotsylvania Court House.

Things you thought you knew #5

NATO never came close to war in Europe with the Warsaw Pact.

"1982 to 1984 was the most dangerous confrontation since the Cuban Missile crisis." The US National Security Agency.

In November 1983 NATO held the five day long Able Archer exercise which was the final phase of the month's long Autumn Forge exercise. What we didn't know at the time was that the Soviets thought Able Archer was not an exercise and that the West was actually preparing a surprise nuclear attack on the Warsaw Pact and intended to follow it with a ground invasion by conventional forces. They were wrong, but their fears were not without good reason.

Part of Able Archer was to practise NATO forces releasing battlefield nuclear weapons in response to a Warsaw Pact chemical attack. Not believing this was an exercise the Soviets got increasingly nervous and put their nuclear forces on high alert and began planning a response to a nuclear first strike by NATO on Eastern Europe.

As you can see below, the Doomsday clock was set at 4 minutes since 1981, at that time the lowest (most dangerous) since the 1950's.

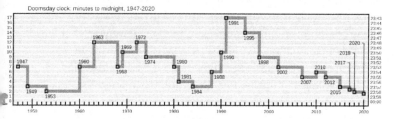

Doomsday clock: minutes to midnight, 1947-2020

Photo credit Fastfission

The Doomsday Clock is a symbol that indicates the probability of a man-made extinction level event like large scale nuclear war or global warming. It has been maintained since 1947 by the members of the Bulletin of the Atomic Scientists and represents the hypothetical global catastrophe as midnight and how close the world is to a catastrophe as how many minutes to midnight.

To understand why the situation developed like it did you have to understand something about the politics of the time and also about the weaponry deployed by East and West. The Cold War was pretty cold at the time, the Soviet invasion of Afghanistan in 1979 effectively ended détente, the Americans boycotted the 1980 Moscow Olympics and the Russians had recently shot down a Korean airliner killing everyone on board. At this time America was tilting towards China diplomatically which made Soviet paranoia about international isolation and being surrounded by enemies even worse than usual.

But there was also a nuclear aspect to the chilliness. In the late seventies the Soviet Union had escalated the arms race by deploying its new SS20 intermediate range nuclear missile on its Western border, a decision they later admitted privately was a mistake. This is a battlefield tactical nuclear missile which can easily reach Western Europe and the Americans responded by deploying their new Pershing II nuclear missiles in Western Europe in 1979, and in the early 80s they deployed cruise missiles. The deployment of the Pershings greatly worried the Russian politburo. They were convinced that the missiles could reach Moscow in 15 minutes, seriously undermining their ability to respond quickly as they would with a ballistic missile launch from submarines or American soil. In actual fact the cruise missiles were a much greater threat as they could hit Moscow within an hour of being launched and were probably undetectable by their radar systems at the time. The first the Russians would have known about it would have been the impact.

To the Russians this was a very threatening move. They had spent decades and millions of roubles that they could ill afford on attempting to keep near parity with American strategic nuclear forces and the deployment of the Pershings and cruise missiles wiped that out. It meant that the West now had the ability to decapitate the Soviet Union and wipe out their ground forces in Eastern Europe at a stroke before they had a chance to respond.

This situation gets more dodgy.

Today the Americans and the Russians have a nuclear weapon policy called 'Launch Under Attack' which means if someone attacks them with nuclear weapons, they will launch their nukes in retaliation. But back then, because of the threat posed by these difficult to detect intermediate range nuclear missiles, both sides had a nuclear weapon policy called 'Launch On Warning'. This means use intelligence to figure out when your adversary is going to launch his weapons and you launch yours *before he launches his*. This policy is of course extremely dangerous, but it means you may just survive the nuclear exchange and there is a small possibility of winning. If you didn't do this you would definitely lose. The nightmare is of course, that it would be easy to mistakenly persuade yourself that your enemy is about to attack you and launch, which is precisely what nearly happened during Able Archer. The situation gets dodgier still.

According to a member of the Soviet general staff at the time, 1983 was the first time since the Second World War that the Soviets practised a nuclear response to intelligence suggesting that the West was going to launch a surprise attack. The Soviet doctrine included pre-emptive nuclear strikes against the western conventional forces build up in Western Europe, so we can be sure that the prospect of an attack from the West was in Soviet planners' minds at the time.

Ronald Reagan's tough stance on the USSR further fuelled the paranoia, describing it as an 'evil empire' and saying he was going to 'consign it to the ash heap of history'. Note the exact words here. Not the *'rubbish heap'* of history, but the *'ash heap'* of history.

Because of the Soviet inability to prevent or even detect the launch of the short range nuclear weapons in Western Europe the Russians set up operation RYaN in 1981. In a secret meeting of senior KGB officers and Soviet political leaders KGB Chairman Yuri Andropov bluntly announced as fact that the United States was preparing a secret nuclear attack on the USSR and to prevent this the KGB and GRU would commence Operation RYaN. (RYaN is a Russian acronym for 'Nuclear Missile Attack'.) This might seem paranoid, but paranoia is something of a Russian speciality, and at this point in time it was less than 40 years since Mother Russia was caught out and almost destroyed by Hitler's surprise Barbarossa offensive in 1941. For operation RYaN the Soviets would rely less on things like satellites and more on its agents in Western countries. These agents monitored a total of 292 different indicators that the West was preparing a surprise nuclear attack. Some of these were sensible, like monitoring nuclear missile sites and senior military and political figures, but some were far-fetched like monitoring blood banks and priests. This, of course, means many random fluctuations can be interpreted as threatening. Ominously, two of the indicators were changes in western military communication systems and changes in how tactical nukes were moved, both of which were changed for Able Archer. The KGB defector Oleg Gordievsky described operation RYaN as, "A vicious circle where Soviet agents abroad were required to report alarming information to Moscow about a surprise nuclear strike even if the agents themselves were sceptical of it". If the agents didn't find any evidence they were told to keep looking until they did. The aspects of Able Archer that brought the Russian leadership's paranoia almost to the boil were many and included radio silence over the relocation of huge numbers of American troops, dummy nuclear weapons being delivered to front line units, NATO aircraft practising nuclear strikes, testing of new communication systems for nuclear release, practising the launch of Pershing and cruise missiles, the shifting of NATO command from Mons to a field headquarters and B2 bomber sorties being mistakenly referred to as nuclear strikes on open radio nets. Some or all of these would have been reported to the politburo by RYaN agents, or heard by Russian radio interceptors.

No one really knows how close the Russians came to implementing the 'Launch on warning' doctrine, but it is a fact that the Warsaw Pact forces prepared extensively for a shooting war by reducing flying hours by aircraft to maximise their availability, putting strategic nukes on alert, redeploying submarines and moving nuclear weapons out of storage and delivering them to front line units by helicopter. The first time the West realised how close we came was a secret British report given to Prime Minister Maggie Thatcher who ordered a minister to 'urgently consider how to approach the Americans with this report to ameliorate the risk of a nuclear miscalculation.' He went, but got the brush off from the American State Department, although about a year later the Americans wrote their own report which echoed almost exactly the British one. For many years after that there were multiple reports in the US government alluding to the danger, but the details of these are still classified. In a fascinating twist, President Ronald Reagan mentioned the near miss in his memoirs and said that 'the world cannot live on a hair trigger'. This pushed him to start talks with the Soviets about reducing nuclear weapons and along with other factors like the collapse of the Russian political system in the early nineties, led to the end of the Cold War.

Personally, I was happily ignorant of the close shave. During Able Archer I was crewing an FV438 that was parked up behind a Schnellimbiss, it cost me a fortune and I put on about half a stone.

Researched and written by Jonno DP.

Fucking tankies!

After Junior Leaders I joined 1RTR at Herford in January 77 and in the early eighties some of my mates and I were sent by the regiment to do an All Arms Demolition course run by the Royal Engineers at Hamel. The course was pretty good, we learnt how to set booby traps, blow up our own vehicles to prevent their capture, drop trees over roads, even how to blow bridges! We were pretty laid back at 1RTR and I expected the same from the Royal Engineers, but no. The instructors insisted on being called Corporal even when we met them out on the piss! This aloof attitude couldn't be maintained with the more easy going approach exhibited by the lads I was on the course with though. One great moment happened when we were practising blowing up a bridge.

The general idea in the event of World War Three was that NATO would go firm on a defensive line, give the Russkies all the punishment they could and then when they got close (which they would as they outnumbered us massively) we would withdraw to another defensive line and do it again, thus slowly bleeding them. As I was reconnaissance, I would always be one of the last over a bridge in a withdrawal. (We always 'withdrew'. The enemy retreats, but we 'withdraw'!)

Now, if you didn't know, all German bridges designed and built after World War Two (which was most of them) already had holes in them to place explosives in the event of a Soviet invasion. They were actually built like this! Many of them would have been blown as soon as World War Three started (preliminary demolitions) and some would have gone up as the Reds advanced (reserve demolitions).

So one sunny day I find myself watching Corporal Upphimself RE demonstrating how to prepare this bridge over a canal for demolition by destroying the pillars if the pre-prepared holes couldn't be used. He repeatedly emphasised the need to keep the det cord tightly wrapped around the structure as it's got much less force if it's not snug up against it. After he finished he gave us parts of the bridge to imitate what he had done and we all picked up the necessary bright blue honeycomb practice explosive, det cord etc and went to work. It looked and felt just like the real thing, it just had extra writing on it to show it was not real high explosive. I clambered over a railing and dangled off the bridge cheerfully looping det cord around girders. While I was working a massive ship started to slide underneath me, chugging quietly along the canal. I stopped a moment to enjoy the peaceful scene thinking how strange it was that the scene was so tranquil, yet I was practising to do something very un-tranquil. I was yanked unceremoniously out of this daydream by the mast at the rear of the barge catching my mates det cord and pulling his whole charge off the bridge, honeycomb explosive, fifty foot of det cord and all, and taking it off down the canal. He didn't even notice until the det cord was sliding through his fingers. I was shocked, but I couldn't stop laughing. Corporal Upphimself noticed me laughing and leant over to ask if everything was ok. "Uhhhhmmmm.........."

We never did get the kit back, and I still wonder what it was like for the barge owner when he looked up and saw something dangling off his mast. Most Germans spoke

225

good English, I just hope his English either wasn't good enough to translate 'explosive' or it was good enough to translate 'inert'. I don't think the Engineers liked us much when we started the course, and I am sure that us all laughing our bollocks off at this didn't increase our popularity.

I think we sealed our regiment's reputation later on when we were felling trees with det cord. In the event of a conflict we might drop trees across roads to slow the enemy advance. I didn't watch the demonstration as carefully as I should have... You are *meant* to wrap about eight inches of det cord around the tree at an angle so the tree falls in the direction of the lowest part. I misunderstood and put eight *feet* of det cord around the tree all at the same height. When I detonated, the bottom half of the tree was blown to matchsticks and the tree went straight up in the air about fifteen feet. It came back down and toppled over in exactly the opposite direction that was required.

It still makes me smile when I think back and remember the RE instructors shouting 'Fucking Tankies!'

'Mumble' Smith 1RTR

A shit idea

In my early thirties I was in A Company the Staffordshire Regiment and one day we were on Sennybridge playing soldiers against the Welsh Guards. We were in a warrior APC doing a TES exercise (the one with lasers) and we had seen, and taken out, two Welsh Guards snipers sneaking through the grass.

We were sat in the warrior when I felt the familiar I-have-been-eating-compo-for-three-days rumble in my stomach. Then, as often happens, it was followed by the sweats. So I said the Mr Burton the one pip wonder that was my platoon commander that I needed to get out and snap one off.

When I was a kid I had a mate called Shotty who had this habit of shitting out of a tree. Fuck it! I thought. Why not? I might be able to see some of those sneaky fucking Guardsmen from up there. So up a tree I went got myself wedged in the V of a branch, arm around the trunk, trousers down, and with a fine view and with the wind wafting the wedding tackle away I went. My mate in the gunners seat looked up and called, "What you doing Shorty?"

"Having a shit."

He started laughing and 2nd Lieutenant Burton poked his head out of the commanders hatch and called out in his posh voice, "Private Shorthouse, what are you doing?"

"Having a shit sir."

"I can see that, but why on earth are you up there?"

The tortoise had his head well out by this time and I was heading for full flow. My mate was still laughing and fell out of his hatch when I said, "Looking for snipers sir".

At the end of the day when the platoon was all back together the lads quizzed me about it and thought it was a great idea. Everyone in the platoon started doing it, then the whole company, then the other companies. Not wanting to be left out other regiments started doing it too, including the Welsh Guards. It kind of caught on a bit like that planking craze a few years ago. By the time we got to Bosnia and Kosovo it was commonplace and people were getting more creative. In Bosnia and Kosovo we had local translators who were amused but absolutely mystified by it. For a while we were working with the Americans and they started doing it as well.

Before sending this story in for the book I told my missus about it and she asked what had possessed me to start a shitting out of a tree craze. To be honest, looking back now it does seem a bit weird, and I can't really remember why I did it, but it seemed funny at the time! I wonder how far the craze spread. I mean, is there a tribesman somewhere in the jungle doing it to the mystification of his mates?

It *did* start to get a bit out of hand though. People starting getting too inventive and doing things like crapping off the back of a Warrior which meant you would jump out and stand in it before you realised. It really went too far when some of the guys started doing it in each other's bins back in camp. You would sneak into someone's room, take the bag out of the bin, shit in it, then put the bag back in. If the recipient wasn't aware of the gag he would look all over the place for the smell, not realising that looking in the empty bin wasn't telling him the full story. Great times!

Michael 'Shorty' Shorthose. A Company, Staffordshire Regiment.

"We few, we happy few, we band of brothers; For he to-day that sheds his blood with me shall be my brother."

King Henry V, prior to the battle of Agincourt (Shakespeare).

HMS Argonaut; One man's story.

My primary reason for joining the Royal Navy as a Marine Engineering Mechanic in February 1981 was my Dad's sage careers advice: "Don't join the Army son, you'll just get blown up in Northern Ireland." Just over a year later I was being bombed and strafed in the Falklands by Argentinians. I don't recall ever thanking him fully.

About 14 months after joining the Navy and completing my training I joined my first ship in late March 1982. She was the Devonport based HMS Argonaut, a Leander class, Exocet armed frigate.

Argonaut had not long come out of an epic five year refit which had been hampered and delayed by a variety of strikes. It should've taken about one year. There were even tee shirts proclaiming 'HMS Argonaut - THE refit'. Little did I realise, we would be returning it to Devonport within three months for another extensive refit for battle damage repair.

I joined just in time to 'enjoy' shakedown at Portland as the ship was becoming operational once more. There was no bunk for me in the Stokers' mess where I should have been, so I was accommodated in the Gunners' mess initially (3EA Mess).

Around this time we heard about the Argentinian scrap metal merchants' antics in South Georgia and later the invasion of the Falkland Islands. Like most people my age (19) I wasn't particularly interested in the news, and like most of the population of Britain, I wondered why Argentina was invading somewhere in Scotland. Geographically challenged as we were, the buzz soon spread – we were going south to link up with the initial task force which had been diverted from Gibraltar. We had a weekend off, store ship in Devonport, then on our way.

It happened so fast, it didn't really sink in. My older brother came to the train station to see me on my way. It occurred to me that it must be something serious for my brother to accompany me to the station.

Upon return to the ship, the mood was buoyant. There was an air of confidence and excitement. One of the Chefs had got married, rumour had it to a prostitute. That seemed more significant than the Argentinian stuff at the time. Besides, the consensus was that they would bugger off once they knew we were on the way.

Argonaut and Ardent escorted 3 Commando

Brigade and the Amphibious Group which included the assault ships Fearless and Intrepid, Royal Fleet Auxiliaries Stromness and Tidepool, the transport Canberra and the oiler Elk.

It all became real on the 2nd of May when the Argentinian ship General Belgrano was sunk. We realised then that there was no going back and we knew the Argentinians would retaliate, we thought by submarine attack. At the time the general feeling was pity for the Argentine sailors who lost their lives, we knew there would be a lot of casualties. We rendezvoused with the initial task group at Ascension Island and joined HMS Ardent in anti-submarine duties around the anchorage, wasting several days chasing submarines that turned out to be whales.

When Sheffield was hit by an Exocet missile, much as it was a shock and a huge blow, it was not unexpected. The worry and frustration we felt was not so much for ourselves, but our families at home who we knew would

231

be very worried and with whom we could not communicate.

The day before the landings was, so far as I remember, grey and overcast and there was a huge rolling swell. As far as the eye could see, there were ships horizon to horizon. The carrier battle group and the amphibious task force looked huge. It looked like a Second World War movie.

On the ship we were briefed in watches in the dining hall by the Captain, who had a map of the islands pinned to a board, and described how the task force would steam initially towards Port Stanley. We were told that the SBS and SAS would conduct a 'son et lumière' (his words) as a diversionary tactic just South of Stanley. The task force would then split and we would jink right, then left, passing between the East and West islands into the amphibious landing area. Our job? Anti-aircraft picket for the amphibious landings at San Carlos.

Our first enemy contact came early on the 21st of May, as we turned into Falkland Sound. An Aermacchi aircraft bounced us firing rockets and cannons injuring the FDO, (our Master at Arms, shot through the chest) and a couple of Gunners on the hangar roof. (One lost an eye, the other had shrapnel through his heel). Due to a breakdown in communications the casualties were brought to the Forward Fire & Repair Party Post instead of the First Aid Post. It shames me to say we initially just stood there aghast at their injuries, frozen in shock, not knowing what to do. Eventually the first aid teams and POMA stabilised the guys and a helicopter was called in to evacuate them and take them ashore. The Master at Arms was eventually taken, I think, to Montevideo, and was extremely lucky to have survived.

The PWO(A) made a sitrep pipe announcing we had our first casualties, saying one of them was the Master at Arms.

'First?' I thought, gloomily.

Initially, we were doing OK. The PWO(A) kept up an excellent running commentary over the main broadcast. We appeared to be hammering the enemy aircraft.

Years later, I spoke with the Commanding Officer of HMS Fearless, now a retired Admiral. He said one of his lasting impressions of the conflict was of Argonaut out in the sound steaming full ahead, firing at the aircraft, a huge white wake behind her. She disappeared behind several massive plumes of water, thrown-up by the bombs that exploded in the water around her and it seemed like a heart stopping eternity before she emerged, unscathed, still firing from behind the spray and mist.

Obviously it was a bit different for us below decks. Those on the upper decks relayed back to us how the battle was going, things like "If you could see the amount of shit we are throwing up at the enemy aircraft, you would feel a lot more confident..."

My inner monologue doubtfully replied, 'Yeah, right'.

The thing I learnt about absolute fear is that it is best left unspoken otherwise it is toxic and highly contagious. Think it, by all means, but never express it until after. The stench of vomit hung in the air below decks; the smell of absolute fear.

The Gunners became the heroes of the day. When you think of it, 260 on the ship, but only a couple of dozen actually firing weapons and missiles. One of the killick Gunners was firing a GPMG and followed the aircraft as it passed overhead. He managed to shoot away one of our whip aerials in his enthusiasm, but hey, most of the bullets were heading in the right direction!

Argonaut claimed a shared hit on an Argentinian Dagger aircraft with HMS Plymouth, and also claimed to have downed a Mirage and an Aermacchi with a Seacat missile unaided on day one alone. That said, with literally hundreds of people pointing weapons in the same direction, it's without doubt that many claimed hits that were at least duplicated. I remember hearing at the time that the tally on the first day of the landings (21 May) over San Carlos was 17 aircraft shot down.

One incident I remember hearing about was that the flight-deck crew got rather jumpy after the first raid, completely understandable in my book. What didn't help however was the gunners tap dancing on the deck of the hangar roof to simulate cannon fire each time an aircraft passed close by. Much to the gunners' mirth, the flight deck crew could be seen diving for cover... until they realised, after which a short, sharp altercation ensued.

One evening I had a walk around the upper deck and was surprised how close we were to land. I thought the islands would just be a blip on each horizon - but there they were - within easy swimming distance. You could even see the Royal Marines on the headlands digging in and establishing defensive positions, should they be required. As we walked around the decks there were dozens and dozens of spent green-painted metal cartridge cases scattered about. At first we thought they were left by our gunners, but they were too big to be from hand held weapons such as GPMGs and too small to be 40/60mm Bofor cartridges. It then dawned on us - they were actually 20mm canon cartridge cases that poured out of the wings of Argentine aircraft as they overflew us, shooting at other targets ahead of them.

The big hit on us came in later that day just as the Casevac helicopter came to the hover over the flight deck. We were huddled outside the Exocet Power Room and had just passed a brew down to the lads in the Seacat magazine and dropped the hatch. We settled back for our own cup of tea and were listening to the Command Loop. We heard the Captain calling "Check" on the weapons systems and the Gunners screaming, "They're Argies, they're Argies". The Captain came back "I repeat, Check, Check..."

Boom! We were hit by two bombs. By some miracle neither exploded.

The Captain got a DSO.

At the moment of the hit my plastic mug of tea (two sugars) catapulted upwards as the deck whipped so everyone got some. At the same time a galvanised steel bucket, brim-full of pee, landed squarely on the head of one of the stokers. Unlucky.

Ever since that day, 21st May 1982, I've never drunk tea as my preferred hot beverage. Superstition? Maybe... but I've not been bombed by an Argentinian Skyhawk since.

After the hit there was a total steam failure and the diesel generators could not be started as the high pressure air system was also ruptured. We were in total darkness. Two guys entered 3EA messdeck and extinguished a small fire. The first one got a mention in despatches.

Whilst this was happening two of us leaped into the pitch black 3EZ messdeck above the magazine and landed knee-deep in diesel fuel. The magazine test plug in the hatch (presumably blocked by debris) indicated no difference in pressure. There was virtually zero visibility - thick white smoke - but no visible fire. We knocked the clips back off the hatch and a solid column of fuel and water spewed about 4 foot upwards. At the time we didn't realise the compartment was open to the sea and as the ship rolled and dipped in the sea the water level inside was equalising with that outside. Try as we might, working with just miners' headlamps to help us see, we couldn't get into the magazine to rescue the guys in there. Later we found out they were killed the instant the bomb came through. We thought we were sinking and four of us stood on the hatch to close it and shore it up with 4"x 4" timber. The water and diesel in the messdecks increased the ship's roll, the force of the liquid actually ripping out bunk and locker fittings making it very dicey for us as they surged across the half flooded compartment whilst we plugged splinter holes on the ship's side

When the bomb hit it had bounced off the starboard side of the magazine, exploding a case of 40/60 Bofor shells, then smashed through a row of Seacat missiles, shearing the warheads off, before coming to rest embedded in the side of the last missile in the row. This was only four or five yards beneath our action station. The hydraulic pressure peeled the deck back and exploded a Seacat missile warhead in the hoist, killing the two sailors in the weapons handling team.

RIP Able Seaman Iain M. Boldy and Able Seaman Matthew J Stuart (Killed on his 18th birthday).

The magazine was flooded by the diesel from the adjacent ruptured fuel tank, miraculously extinguishing the blaze.

Below the waterline entry hole of the bomb
that lodged in Argonauts Seacat magazine.

Smashed Seacat missiles stored in their magazine under fibreglass covers before we started to lift out the wreckage.

The second bomb had come through on the waterline, flooding the boiler room as the crew escaped. It took away the top of the turbo alternator (generator), the high pressure air ring main, split the engine-room/boiler room bulkhead, smashed the high pressure saturated steam pipe and stopped the blower which was feeding air to the port boiler. The boiler imploded and exploded but the casings held it together. This caused a total power failure, all lights were out, but the Chief Stoker managed to plug the holes using a sledgehammer and wooden wedges. It wasn't until the damage repair party shone a battery powered floodlight into the compartment that the Chief

Stoker realised he was swinging a sledgehammer whilst actually stood on top of the UXB.

HMS Argonaut 1,000lb UXB in the boiler room My mattress was used to stop it rolling (top right)

The boiler room crew had escaped into the Tech Office directly above, tripping the boilers as they exited. The room was filled with steam from a burst pipe smashed by the bomb and flooded through the hole in the ship's side. The chefs in the Galley managed to haul the stokers through the escape hatch. One of them was a big lad, who we had always joked wouldn't have fitted through an escape hatch. He did, with a bit of steam propulsion to help him on his way, broiling his backside. Everyone in the vicinity later swore they felt their ears pop as he emerged. After the bombs hit, the ship was out of control ploughing full ahead toward Fanning Head because the engine and boiler room had been evacuated. A young Sub Lieutenant called Morgan ran from the bridge to the foc'sle and slipped the anchor bringing us to a juddering halt. The same guy later dived in the flooded magazine to check whether the bomb had passed clean through – it hadn't, as I said, it was lodged in the magazine. He also sighted the bodies. A very brave chap, he actually had to take off his diving set and pass it through the bomb entry holes first so he could swim after it. The next 24 hours were spent trying to strip out the messdecks whilst we were towed further into San Carlos Bay by a couple of Fearless' landing craft.

That evening HMS Plymouth, our heroes of the hour amidst the action, tied-up alongside us as we anchored providing us with food and passing air lines to try and get a generator going. Immediately after the hit, Plymouth put herself between the aircraft and ourselves, throwing up a barrage of 4.5-inch shells, effectively stopping a coup de grâce.

Argonaut was silent. No power, no ventilation noise, battery lighting, and you could hear each footfall echoing around the ship. Very eerie. Later the damage repair patrol laughingly reported back to the section base that they had caught an MEM called Spider (name changed to protect the guilty), wearing a miners' headlamp in the switchboard reading an adult magazine.

Several hours later, there was a click on the main

broadcast system, followed by a pause. To a man we waited expectantly - was it going to be a sitrep? Presumably internal comms had switched it onto battery back-up. A whispered, quizzical deep voice boomed around the ship in a stage whisper, "Spider......? Spider......? We're watching you Spider......" Muffled pockets of laughter could be heard throughout the ship. The sheet aluminium tail section of the boiler room bomb had separated from the main charge. Later, several stokers cut bits off the sheet metal and made bomb-shaped highly polished pendants as mementos 2 to 3 centimetres long. I later ditched mine. Who'd want a bloody bomb-shaped pendant anyway, I reasoned.

As I said earlier, the first UXB was lodged nose first in a Seacat missile, submerged in diesel and could not be made safe. The task of removal meant plugging the submerged entry hole, recovering the bodies, pumping out the compartment, removing the missiles, cutting holes above the bomb, securing the bomb, then cutting a hole in the ship's side to hoist it out and lower it into the sea. After that, weld plates over the holes.

Me and my oppo Jonah were tasked with pumping water out of the flooded magazine. We eventually got the Salvage pump onto the foc'sle (another later arriving by helicopter from Fearless), and lowered the suction hose two decks through the foc'sle hatch into the flooded magazine directly below. Whilst starting the pump the two of us were winding the turbine like crazy. The noise, perhaps not surprisingly, was like a jet engine, so we didn't hear the pipe, "Air Raid Red".

At the same moment we both realised there was a loud noise other than the one we were making and we looked up. We saw an Argentine Dagger aircraft no more than fifty foot directly above us flying belly-first on the apex of a sharp turn, afterburner screaming raw noise at us, empty spent cartridge shells spilling out and literally landing all around us as it cannoned another ship in its sights. The two bombs he had aimed at Argonaut exploded underwater in a kind of stuttered 'ba-boom' not 25 yards away on each side. Two huge columns of water exploded upwards either side of the foc'sle, completely drenching us with icy water. The two of us stood gaping at each other, hair plastered on our heads, soaked through, unable to talk. I was thinking to myself, 'Jeez, that was a bit close'.

Jonah, on the other hand, was elated. "That was fucking brilliant!" he mouthed with no audible sound. By the way, the experts state that during an explosion you should open your mouth to equalise the pressure wave and protect your eyes. In reality you instinctively achieve this by screwing your eyes shut whilst screaming an expletive. Job done.

As the whistling hiss of temporary deafness subsided we could hear an angry bloke shouting at us in the distance and getting closer. It was the Chief Stoker who had come up onto the soaked deck, kicking empty cartridge cases angrily out of his path, to find out why we hadn't started the pump.

"Stop fucking loafing you two!" He shouted.

Eventually we had two pumps running in the hope we could pump out faster than the water was coming in, but all they were doing was recirculating the South Atlantic by drawing water through the three foot wide bomb entry hole and pumping it out again.

It was decided to plug the holes to the sea, remove as much fuel and water as possible, then hand over to the Fleet Clearance Diving team for the removal of the bomb. The shipwrights from Fearless came over to assist as we needed to cut an evacuation route in the deck of 3EZ mess, then another in the PO's mess above, then a third in the ship's side in the PO's mess. To cut the bomb route we had to strip the messdeck and PO's mess bare, the debris simply being float tested. It took 40 hours, without sleep, to stabilise the effects of the damage and contain it fore and aft.

We recovered the bodies as we began to pump out the magazine in earnest. They were placed in the paint shop right at the forward end of the ship and later handed over with due ceremony to HMS Plymouth who did us the great honour of committing them to the deep.

There was a lot of anger and resentment on the lower decks regarding the loss of our shipmates and this flared up particularly when we recovered the second body. One member of the ship's company took it upon himself to 'have a word' with the Captain. Perhaps fortunately, he stormed into the empty day cabin rather than the occupied night cabin and was intercepted by the POMA who was also Acting Master at Arms. Whether the Captain ever heard what was shouted about him I'll probably never know, but we hoped he did.

At the time of recovering our casualties, both of our Hong-Kong Chinese laundrymen learned that in the event of an Exocet attack, the tactic was to turn the port quarter of the ship to face the incoming missile, to minimise the target area and limit the operational damage potential. Bear in mind that at this point we had no fresh water available for things like washing clothes so it was not vital that they remained in that zone during the daily Action Stations. The laundry was in the port quarter that would face any incoming missiles and needless to say, the laundry staff were understandably perturbed about this. They began a search to find somewhere else to be, out of harm's way. As luck didn't have it, as no-one had thought to tell the poor chaps, they stumbled into our temporary mortuary. If they were worried before, they were even more worried now.

Later on the divers took out the whole missiles from the Seacat magazine one by one, whilst the repair party gingerly picked up the remaining bits and pieces and lobbed them overboard. When the divers finished for the day the magazine was deliberately re-flooded.

As the Chippy (shipwright) was cutting the hole in the deck in the PO's mess an aircraft again strafed us, fully visible to him through the large hole in the side of the mess. Not surprisingly the Chippy dived for cover but his welding torch set fire to the diesel film that covered everything causing a blaze took us about an hour and a half to extinguish. Remember this was on top of the diesel flooded magazine with a UXB and damaged missiles under the surface. Nice.

The firefighting team I was in to fight this fire had two hoses. One was a waterwall operator at the front, followed by the firefighter (me) and a team leader behind, driving the team forward. The waterwall is literally a flat disk of water coming out of a fire hose at 90 degrees to protect the fire-fighting team. The fire-fighter fires a jet (or more correctly 'ragged spay') through the waterwall to extinguish the blaze. As we moved forward in the cramped passageway with the water-wall operator in the lead he was getting pretty hacked off with me inadvertently bouncing the firefighting jet of water off his head. I couldn't see him through the spray and smoke and thermal imaging cameras weren't used then. There was fire everywhere, with no obvious source. What we found out later was that the explosive had leached out of the missiles and a film of diesel covered everything. What we thought were salt crystals were actually explosive, hence the heat of the fire. The light fittings and cable insulation melted onto our heads as we moved forward. The only head protection we had was anti-flash hoods, no comms in those days. The breathing apparatus (ICABA) lasted about sixteen minutes, half that when you were breathing like a runaway locomotive with molten plastic dripping on your head. This was accompanied by bloody great blue flashes and resounding bangs as we passed each 440 volt transformer which we were filling with water from the water wall.

As if fighting a fire atop a diesel flooded missile magazine wasn't exciting enough, as we passed the PO's bunk space and advanced forward, a guy burst out of his section base dispersal point. He was completely disorientated, shouting rather excitedly, coughing and spluttering, but nonetheless rather pleased to see us. He made me jump out of my skin, I wasn't expecting a loony. I grabbed him, pushed him behind us and shouted through the noise of the fire hoses.

"Follow our hoses out of the compartment".

We carried on. A few moments later he was back coughing and spluttering in my starboard lughole. Jeez, a 50-50 chance of following the fire-hoses in the right direction away from the big, orange, flickery, hot thing and he got it wrong! What a pain, can't he see we're bloody busy? Probably not. Passing my hose to the team leader, I squeezed past and encouraged him in the right direction by literally kicking his butt time and again until he got through the smoke boundary door. Oddly, I met the guy again several years later whilst serving on HMS Boxer. He always thanked me profusely when the beer started flowing! Strange chap. My response was "Anytime you want pointing in the right direction Vic, give me a shout, no worries".

As I got back with the team, the warning whistles started sounding on the breathing apparatus and we began to withdraw as a team from aft arrived to take over. In those days, we only had about eight BA sets and half a dozen spare air bottles for the whole ship. As I exited the door one of the officers snatched my BA set and demanded a hot bottle change. He then decided to enter the smoke filled compartment by getting the upper deck crews to lower him on a rope over the ship's side, where he then swung through the hole cut into the ship's side, as you do. Doors obviously weren't good enough for this bloke. His mission was to find out what was happening. He only needed to ask us and we would have told him. To cap it off, he exited via the foc'sle hatch and went up to the bridge to brief the Captain. Presumably, it ran along the lines of: "Erm, lots of smoke and fire, sir. Very hot".

Around about this time we had a short visit from some Royal Marine SBS lads who had been in the thick of it. They were merely cross-decking and now we had power restored they took the opportunity to have a hot shower and food. They looked tired, and a few of them joined us for a smoke and a chance to relax a little. They didn't realise we still had a couple of unexploded bombs on board until we mentioned it and they were surprised at how seemingly unperturbed we were about that state of affairs.

"Worse things happen at sea, Royal." someone smiled.

The special forces lads said they felt they preferred being able to see the enemy and being able to shoot at them rather than stuck in a tin box, not knowing what was going on outside with the chance of something crashing through the side at any moment. Until it was actually expressed, I hadn't thought of it this way, but they certainly had a valid point.

A day or so later the Chief Stoker decided he was going to have a play with a ramset explosive rivet gun to patch the waterline hole in the boiler room. The plan was to lower him over the ship's side on the end of a man-overboard strop dressed in a diving suit whilst clutching an aluminium deck plate which he was going to rivet over the entry hole with the gun.

In hindsight, when using a ramset explosive rivet gun, you would be well advised to try smallest explosive cartridge first, rather than the biggest.

As it was, a few rivets were blasted into the ship, clean through the deckplate and ship's side then ricocheted, with a satisfying cowboy western movie ping-ah around the boiler room several times before the right sized charge was finally found. Enjoying himself immensely I could picture the loon with the gun whistling the opening bars of The Good, The Bad and The Ugly after each 'Ker-bang-ping...ring-a-ding'.

"If an air attack comes in lads," the Chief Stoker shouted,

cheerily swinging on his bit of rope and looking upwards to the four of us holding onto him, the rope held with a single turn on a cleat, "Just lower me gently into the water." Next minute, the main broadcast crackled, "Air Raid Warning Red! Air Raid Warning Red!" followed by a big splash about six feet beneath the place where the Chief Stoker had previously dangled.

"Bastards" we heard him splutter as we closed the screen door hammering on the clips to get a bit of steel between ourselves, a brace of incoming hostile aircraft and an equally hostile Chief Stoker.

After the air raid was over and we had recovered the stoker the focus shifted to removing the magazine bomb, still live, with its nose wedged inside a Seacat missile. It was decided to get as many people off the ship as possible during this operation due to the very real risk of explosion. HMS Fearless' Landing craft lifted off 75% of Argonaut's crew and ferried them onto Fearless whilst the magazine bomb was removed from the forward magazine by the Fleet Clearance Diving Team. The remaining quarter of the ship's company (2nd of Port Watch) hoisted the bomb in a series of pulleys from the flight deck, whilst the bomb disposal team guided it through the series of holes cut through the ship by the Shipwrights from HMS Fearless. Two people had to stay below in the boiler room the bomb was wedged in, keeping the starboard boiler going. The two were Petty Officer Phil Phillips and, as luck didn't have it, me. A series of fuel chain tanks linked the boiler-room to the magazine, so if the bomb had exploded, we wouldn't have known much about it.

By this time the air threat at night had diminished, and was limited to inaccurate high level bombing by Canberra aircraft. But of a night all ships anchored in San Carlos were potentially vulnerable to attack from divers planting limpet mines etc, so scare charges were set off to deter them. A scare charge, if you don't know, is an explosive 14 ounce charge similar to a hand-grenade, but twice the size.

Before they started hoisting the bomb Phil placed a couple of damage control wooden wedges on the deck.

"What are they for?" I remember asking, puzzled.

"Well, if that thing goes pop, they're my starting blocks. I want a head start getting out of that hatch before you" smiled Phil reassuringly.

As the bomb was hoisted, the main broadcast tannoy was used to control the hoisting team. As it was lowered onto the waterline and the announcement was made over the tannoy, "Bomb on the water," a scare charge exploded very close by.

I beat Phil to the top of the hatch, no problem, just before the third 'o' in the 'ker-boooooom'.

Meanwhile, whilst we looked inward to our ship, licking our wounds, reports were coming in of other ships being hit all around us. The news wasn't good. We were losing, it was felt. An aircraft dropping a bomb on Antelope clipped her main mast and crashed (I think).

We went up on deck to watch Antelope steam silently into the anchorage, mast askew, a black smudge on the ship's side where the bomb had entered killing a member of the ship's company but not exploding. Yet. We clapped and cheered her as she anchored-up awaiting the arrival of the army bomb disposal team.

The 500lb bomb in Antelope detonated whilst being defused by Staff Sergeant Jim Prescott CGM (RIP) Royal

Engineers, who had defused Argonaut's boiler room bomb a few days earlier.

After the initial explosion the fire on Antelope raged all night. We were anchored quite close, still crippled. The Royal Marines again came to our aid in their landing-craft and towed us about 400 yards away from the blazing ship. They then went on to help lift off the crew from Antelope when the order was given to abandon ship and Argonaut's whaler seaboat lifted off about 20 of Antelope's crew. Eventually her Seacat magazine exploded and the ship broke in two, sinking the next day.

I've never had much time for those who say they saw combat but never talk about it. Odds are they maybe were never asked or possibly nowt happened worth mentioning, so for them less is more with regards kudos, if that's what they seek. Perhaps the worry is that if you ask, you cannot shut the boring sod up. For me, immediately after the Falklands my decompression therapy was talking about it, hence the fact all my family have permanently glazed expressions, poor buggers.

Anyway, back to then. We eventually got steam up in the unaffected starboard boiler and were able to steam out toward the repair ship, Stena Seaspread, outside the TEZ to the East of the islands. Frankly, they were brilliant, they could not do enough to help. The ship's crew were largely Royal Navy and they were staggered by the damage to Argonaut and frustrated they were not fighting also. Had they asked at the time, I'd have happily swapped.

After the conflict Argonaut went into dry dock and it became apparent there was more damage than had been thought. The keel had bowed, damaged by the underwater blast of near-miss bombs that exploded in the water around us, the superstructure welds were splitting away from the deck due to the twisting action of the South Atlantic ocean swell and down aft canon holes were discovered on the underside of the propellor guards which explained why we couldn't find any damage when we heard the canon shells hitting us there.

Eventually we started steaming north toward Ascension Island and home. The war still had a week or so to run, but the daily air threat to shipping was gone, or so we thought. We had steamed east a long way, out of the reach of Argentine aircraft, almost as far away as the aircraft carriers and their escorts, just off the African coast.

(Editor's note; He is being sarcastic about the location of the Aircraft Carriers here, but he has a point. Sandy Woodward commanding the Task Force was heavily criticised after the conflict for keeping the Aircraft Carriers, and therefore the Harriers too far away, thus reducing the effectiveness of British air cover. The journalist Max Hastings even suggested the crews of the carriers get an Africa Star instead of a Falklands medal.)

One evening we were unexpectedly called to action stations at the rush. The sound of the main broadcast alarm still bloody haunts me, jarring on my nerves, calling my mind back. That, and the pervasive smell of diesel fuel. We had spent days wading around in the stuff and I swear it actually gets absorbed into your skin. I could still smell it for several days after I got home, no matter how much I washed.

The main broadcast crackled to life, "Air Raid Red, Air Raid Red". We trudged rather than ran, utterly dejected after thinking we had finally, finally escaped with our lives. We hadn't. This was it. People could be heard retching with fear again.

"Agave radar detected, sixty miles, closing from the west". No-one spoke. We didn't need to. We knew. Exocet.

The ship went into a juddering turn to place the port beam toward the threat and we leant over with the ship much like riding pillion on a motorcycle. Odd that, never really thought about it, but you do just that on a ship at speed. Then, completely unexpectedly,

"Target splashed".

The relief was phenomenal. Disbelief, dumbstruck, instant joy. Beer was needed. Burp.

What actually happened I cannot fully recall, but later reports said it was a raid by four Skyhawks and two Etendards on the two British aircraft carriers. Due to a clever deception by the captain of the Hermes, the Argies had miscalculated the position of his ship by thirty miles and flew straight into the screen defending it. HMS Arrow claimed it had shot a missile shot down with its 4.5-inch gun, but the missile may have just run out of fuel. Exeter shot down two of the Skyhawks and the other two Skyhawks attacked her, dropping bombs that missed before returning to base. When debriefed, the pilots of these two Skyhawks claimed that they had bombed the carrier HMS Invincible and left her a burning wreck. Exeter was the only other Royal Navy ship carrying the same air warning radar as Invincible and coupled with the smoke from Exeter's missile launches the Argie pilots may have believed that they had bombed the Carrier. Apparently there is currently a painting of Invincible in flames hanging

252

in the Argie pilot's aircrew room! But then, there were Argie Skyhawks with "Argonaut" painted on their nose and we weren't sunk either!

Victory markings on an Argentine Skyhawk for the sinking of the three British warships Argonaut, Antelope, and Ardent. Except Argonaut wasn't sunk.

After that, we continued to arc north. One thing I do recall was a report saying HMS Plymouth had been hit by several bombs and to a man we wanted to go back to assist. Plymouth were our saviours, we owed them one. As it happened help was close at hand so we reluctantly continued sailing north.

The next thing to happen to me was better than winning

the lottery and luckier than being only a few yards from a bomb that should have killed many of us. About a quarter of us had our names drawn out of a hat as we approached Ascension. We were being flown home! Advance leave party, with only a day's notice. It hadn't even occurred to me that this might happen, but the ticket was priceless. We disembarked on a Mexeflote, blinking in the tropical sun, just a grip permitted for baggage. It was unreal. The VC10 also had some of the casualties from HMS Sheffield and HMS Coventry who were already on the aircraft.

On the flight a group of us from the north had decided we would hire a minibus between us so we could get home. Obviously, there was no way of us communicating with the UK, so we decided that after we arrived at an empty at RAF Brize Norton at 0200 we would have a kip somewhere until the car hire office opened in the morning and then we would be on our way.

A cheer went up as we landed and we taxied toward the terminal in the dead of night. The casualties were taken off first, then we disembarked.

To our complete astonishment the terminal building was full of people, lots of people. Hundreds of them waving and cheering, cameras flashing.

What????

It's 2am, no-one knows we are coming home.

We kept looking around to see who was the centre of all this attention. Was Michael Jackson or Elton John arriving too? Nope.

As we entered the building, the base commander welcomed us all back and said those fateful words, "As far as I'm concerned, you've now cleared customs, lads". There was a resounding "bastard" muttered in unison. The Naval Regulators had warned us all not to buy any booze at Ascension as it would be confiscated upon arrival. The RAF, bless 'em, couldn't have cared less. Bugger.

We northerners got our bags and huddled together ready to make our exit through the waiting crowds and find somewhere to wait for the hire place to open. The crowds would've been for the casualties, and rightly so.

Wrong.

As we entered the arrivals hall, one by one the lads saw people they knew and peeled-off. And there, stood in front of me, unbelievably, was my Mum, tears streaming down her face. All she had seen up to that point were casualties, bless her, and I wasn't one of them.

Rob Lockyer

"I could not tread these perilous paths, if I did not have a sense of humour."

Admiral Horatio Nelson.

Well, they were the stories I was sent, hopefully you enjoyed reading them as much as I did. If a memory of yours has been stirred and you fancy having a bit of immortality in volume 3 please email it to me at damonjohnson@zoho.com. If you would prefer you can email me a phone number and I will give you a ring. At the time of writing this I have enough material for about half of book 3, so room for more! All stories that I have that didn't appear in volume 2 will definitely appear in volume 3, apologies for not putting them in, but time caught up with me. I reckon volume three will be done before the end of 2021 and if you want to get email notification of when it comes out click on 'Follow Author' on the amazon page for this book.

If you enjoyed this book please consider giving it a rating (or even a review) on Amazon. Now if you will excuse me, the boxset of Miss Marple has arrived for the missus and I had better get on with volume 3...

Glossary

2ic. Second in command.

432. See FV432.

AAC. Army Air Corps.

Active edge. During the Cold War British Forces would do emergency deployments to counter a surprise attack by the Eastern Bloc. The phone would ring (usually in the middle of the night) and you would hear the code words "Active Edge". This was traditionally followed by a few minutes swearing by the message recipient and laughter by the message giver. Then you would ring someone else and the roles would be reversed.

AFV. Armoured Fighting Vehicle.

Ally. A word which describes how cool someone or their equipment looks.

APC. Armoured Personnel Carrier.

Apotheke. The German word for a pharmacy.

ARV. Armoured Recovery Vehicle.

ASM. Artificer Sergeant Major. The senior non officer in a **REME unit**. Like an RSM but more oily.

AVRE. Armoured Vehicle Royal Engineers.

BA. Breathing apparatus.

Bahnhof. Station

BAOR. British Army On the Rhine.

Basha. A temporary shelter put up to sleep in and/or to provide protection from the elements, often consisting of just a single sheet of waterproof material. The origin is from Assamese and probably first entered the British Army vocabulary with Chindits operating behind enemy lines in Burma.

BATUS. British Army Training Unit Suffield. A huge (and I do mean HUGE) training area in Canada. Pro tip – don't go digging there. Everyone and his uncle have buried ammunition there by the ton.

Bergen. Backpack.

BFT. Battle Fitness Test or Basic Fitness Test, depending on which PTI is screaming at you.

BSM. Battery Sergeant Major.

B vehicles. Lorries, land rovers etc. The bigger stuff was called A vehicles.

CALM. Crane Atlas Lorry Mounted.

Casevac. Casualty evacuation.

Cloud puncher. Anti-Aircraft missile operator.

CO. Commanding Officer. Usually a Lieutenant Colonel.

Colchester. The town were the British military prison was. The prison was called 'The Military Training and Correction Centre or just MCTC, but someone wouldn't usually use that term, they would just say, "He spent a month in Colchester".

Comcen. Communications centre.

Crab air. The phrase used by the British army to denote the air wing of the royal navy. The Navy are called 'Crabs' by the Army.

CSM. Company Sergeant Major.

Det cord. Detonation cord. It looks like, and is about the same size as coax cable, but it's a plastic sheath filled with explosive.

DTG. Data Telegraphist.

Extras. Extra duties given as a punishment for a minor disciplinary issue, or for victimisation purposes.

FDO. Flight Deck Officer.

Float tested. A navy euphemism for throwing something away over the side of the ship.

Foc's'le. The forward deck of the ship. It derives its name from the days of sailing ships when the raised forward deck was known as the 'forecastle'.

FRT. Forward Repair Team.

FTX. Field Training Exercise.

Full webbing. The belt, pouches, straps etc that soldiers have to wear to carry their kit in. It may or may not include a bergen (backpack) as well. It's heavier than you think.

FV432. An Armoured Personnel Carrier with a wide range of variants. (FV stands for Fighting Vehicle).

FV434. The variant of the FV432 armoured personnel carrier that mechanics crewed.

FV438. A variant of the FV432, equipped with swingfire missiles.

Gat. Army slang for a small arm.

GCP. German Civil Police. Known by the German population as 'Bulle', which is the German word for Bulls, (In the same way as the British used to use the word 'Pigs') due to their reputation for an unsophisticated approach and tendency to hurt people.

GPMG. General Purpose Machine Gun. A belt fed light machine gun. Also known as a 'Jimpy' or 'Gimpy'.

Gunner. The Artillery's equivalent of the rank of Private.

HQ. Headquarters.

ICBM. Inter-Continental Ballistic Missile.

Jimpy. See GPMG.

Joe Baxi. Taxi.

KGB. Committee for State Security. The main Russian spy organisation.

Killick. Navy slang for a leading seaman. Comes from the nautical term meaning a heavy stone used by small craft as an anchor.

LAD. Light Aid detachment. The small group of mechanics and vehicle electricians that accompany a squadron, company, battery etc.

Lance Jack. Slang for a lance corporal.

Lasing a target. Using a laser rangefinder to find the range.

LCpl. Abbreviation for Lance Corporal.

Lid. Helmet.

Matloes. Or Matelows or Matelots. British slang for sailors in the Royal navy.

MCTC. See 'Colchester'.

MEM. Marine Engineering Mechanic.

Mexeflote. A landing raft to move goods and vehicles between ship and shore.

MP. Military Police. More properly called RMP, Royal Military Police.

MSR. Main Supply Route.

MT. Motor Transport.

NAAFI. Navy Army Air Force Institute. Shop/bar most camps have in some shape or form.

NBC. Nuclear Bacterial Chemical.

NCO. Non-Commissioned Officer. Lance Corporal up to Sergeant Major.

ND. Negligent Discharge. (Of a weapon). In other words, firing it when you didn't mean to. Very bad news if you did it. There used to be a lesser 'Accidental discharge', but it was decided that Accidental Discharges were negligent. So that's nice.

NI gloves. Northern Ireland gloves. Decent padded leather gloves that replaced 'Gloves, green, woollen.' Someone in authority finally realised that these wool gloves were crap. They were ok for keeping your hands warm, but they had serious shortcomings. For example, try handling a gloss painted artillery shell weighing nearly 50 kilos when wearing woolly gloves without dropping it. Dropping shells filled with high explosive is generally frowned upon if you didn't know.

Nig. Nothing racist but you always hear everyone suddenly go quiet when you use it around civvies. It means New Intake Group; a derogatory term meaning a soldier, or group of soldiers recently arrived from basic training. If a soldier hadn't been out of training long, he would be described as 'niggy'. You would sometimes see soldiers with over a decade's service arguing about who was least niggy.

Noddy kit. NBC suit.

OC. Officer Commanding. The officer in charge of a Squadron, Company or Battery. Usually a Major.

OPSEC. OPerational SECurity.

OR's. Other Ranks; in descending order the list goes; Officers, Senior NCO's, Junior NCO's, Other Ranks. The term Other Ranks is used rather than Private because it includes Sappers, Chefs etc which is what Privates are called in the Engineers, Catering Corps and so on.

Ord. Ordnance.

Pad/pads. Married soldiers.

Pepperpotting. When closing on the enemy position, the team breaks down into pairs for better angles of suppression, and this technique is referred to as 'pepper-potting'.

Petty Officer. Navy equivalent of a Sergeant.

Pit. Bed.

Plates of meat. Feet.

POMA. Petty Officer Medical Assistant.

Pongo. Navy and RAF slang term for the British Army. 'Where the Army goes the pong goes.'

Provo. Regimental police.

Prowler. Part of the guard that patrols a camp at random to deter intruders.

PTI. Physical Training Instructor. Bastards to a man. If you are not the sort of person that likes torturing kittens don't join, you won't fit in. Huge, hard, nasty. Actually, I think that might be their motto.

PTI shouting out 1022...1023...1024.... PTIs would count down the last few seconds if you were about to fail your BFT, which you would if you took longer than 10 minutes 30 seconds (depending on your age).

PWO. Principal warfare officer.

Q. Quartermaster.

QM. Also means quartermaster.

QRF. Quick Reaction Force.

Queen's regulations. A doorstep sized book that contains British Military law. I don't think anyone has ever read it, and that includes lawyers, but then, there's no need to. When the Army wanted to shaft you, it was usually under article 69a. This was 'Conduct to the Prejudice of Good Order and Military Discipline'. A catch all rule. They didn't like the way you breathed? You were bringing the army into disrepute! Mind yer fingers, CLANG!

R&R. Rest and Recuperation. Theoretically a time for personnel to rest and recuperate. In reality; "LETS GET PISSED!!!!!!"

Ramset gun. A powder-actuated tool (often generically called a Hilti gun or a Ramset gun after their manufacturing companies) is a type of nail gun used in construction and manufacturing to join materials to hard substrates such as steel and concrete.

RAOC. Recruit Any Old Cunt. Sorry! Royal Army Ordnance Corp.

RCT. Rickshaws Cabs and Taxis. Sorry! Royal Corps of Transport.

RE. Royal Engineers.

REME. Ruin Everything Mechanical Eventually. Sorry! Royal Electrical and Mechanical Engineers.

REMF. Rear Echelon Mother Fucker. This one I do mean.

Ressie. Respirator.

RGJ. Royal Green Jackets. An Infantry regiment with a fierce reputation.

RHQ. Regimental Headquarters.

RLC. Royal Logistics Corps.

RNAS. Royal Naval Air Station.

RO2. Radio Operator 2nd class.

Rodneys. Derogatory army term for officers. Ruperts is also used, and they are often pronounced as Wodneys and Wooperts.

ROP's. Restriction Of Privileges. When they don't jail you but still want to fuck you around. Basically, it meant you did shitty jobs in the evening and weekends and were paraded several times a day to increase the fuck-around-factor. Your Dad and mine called it Jankers.

RP. Regimental Police.

RSM. Regimental Sergeant Major. The most senior Non Commissioned Officer in a unit. A man to be feared, and if possible avoided.

RTR. Royal Tank Regiment.

SAC. Senior Aircraftsman.

SAS. Special Air Service.

SBS. Special Boat Service.

Schnellimbiss. German fast foot establishment.

Scimitar/Scorpion. A light tank used for reconnaissance.

Sigs. Signals.

Sitrep. Situation report.

SLR. Self Loading Rifle. A semi-automatic rifle issued to British forces from the early fifties to the early nineties.

SMG. Sterling sub machine gun. Little known fact. In Star Wars films Imperial Troopers blasters were based on this weapon with the butt folded.

Son et lumière. An entertainment held by night at a historic monument or building, telling its history by the use of lighting effects and recorded sound.

SOP. Standard Operating Procedure.

SOXMIS. Properly called 'Soviet Military Mission to BAOR'. This was an organisation that operated in West Germany with the knowledge and consent of the Western allies. The other three powers (America, France and Britain) had similar missions. The idea was that each side would know if the other was mobilising for war and so false alerts that may lead to a real war would be avoided. Obviously, the opportunity was taken by all sides to spy on each other.

SSM. Surface to Surface Missile or Squadron Sergeant Major. Quite easy to tell apart. One is a fast moving object that can explode when you are not expecting it, and the other one is a Surface to Surface Missile.

Stag. Duty, for example if it's your turn to go and stand in the rain in a muddy trench you are 'on stag'.

Stally. A Stalwart. A very versatile semi armoured lorry with swimming capability that was used to carry kit/fuel/ammunition. Probably the best vehicle ever issued to the British Army.

TES. Tactical Engagement Simulation. Soft lasers are fitted to small arms and receivers are placed on the soldiers bodies so a realistic shoot out can be had by all.

TEZ. Total Exclusion Zone.

Tick tocking. Marching like a clockwork soldier.

Troopie. Troop Commander.

TSM. Troop Sergeant Major.

Ulu. The middle of nowhere.

UXB. UneXploded Bomb.

VC10. Troop carrying Aircraft.

VM. Vehicle Mechanic.

Wanking chariot. The bed of someone you consider a wanker.

WO2. Warrant Officer 2nd Class.

WRAC. Women's Royal Army Corps, or Warm Round And Cuddly. There were other versions of the letters WRAC, but I am not saying.

If you enjoyed this book, I recommend this one by Harry Clacy...

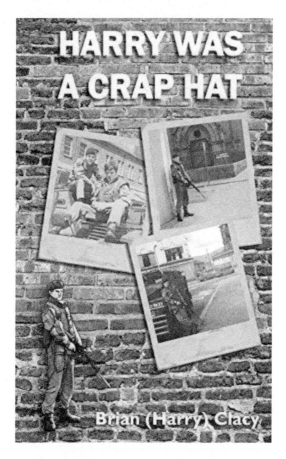

Harry was a Crap Hat - (Second Edition) At the age of sixteen I joined the British Army with every intention of winning a Victoria Cross for saving my unit from certain death...

Printed in Great Britain
by Amazon

22856497R00155